W9-ABY-070

FRANK LLOYD WRIGHT
THE BUILDINGS

FRANK LLOYD WRIGHT
THE BUILDINGS

PHOTOGRAPHS BY ALAN WEINTRAUB | TEXT BY ALAN HESS

With contributions by David G. De Long and Kathryn Smith

Rizzoli
NEW YORK

HUXLEY PUBLIC LIBRARY

For Michael Bernstein

— AW

For Tim and Lindsay

— AH

First published in the United States of America in 2008 by
RIZZOLI INTERNATIONAL PUBLICATIONS, INC.
300 Park Avenue South
New York, NY 10010
www.rizzoliusa.com

ISBN-13: 978-0-8478-3093-0
Library of Congress Control Number: 2008922994

Photography (except when otherwise noted throughout book) © 2008 Alan Weintraub/ Arcaid@arcaid.co.uk

Text (except as indicated below) © 2008 Alan Hess

"Reshaping Urban Landscapes" © 2008 David G. De Long

"Frank Lloyd Wright: Selected Plans" © 2008 Kathryn Smith

© 2008 Rizzoli International Publications

Pages 58 (photograph), pp. 234–249: The image of the Solomon R. Guggenheim Museum is a trademark of The Solomon R. Guggenheim Foundation. Used by permission.

Photography, drawings, and other artwork not credited here are credited, when appropriate, in the section in which such images appear.

All rights reserved. No part of this publication may be reproduced, stored in a retrieval system, or transmitted in any form or by any means, electronic, mechanical, photocopying, recording, or otherwise, without prior consent of the publisher.

Distributed to the U.S. trade by Random House, New York

Designed by Zand Gee

Printed and bound in China

2008 2009 2010 2011 2012/ 10 9 8 7 6 5 4 3 2 1

Jacket cover: Taliesin West, 1937
Jacket back: Marin County Civic Center, 1957
p. 2: Marin County Civic Center, 1957
pp. 6–7: Unity Chapel, Taliesin North, 1886
pp. 62–63: Marin County Civic Center, 1957
p. 312: Taliesin North, 1886

The Buildings

Contents

Frank Lloyd Wright: Buildings for the City

By Alan Hess

The first Frank Lloyd Wright design to be built was one with a public purpose:
a small family chapel on his family's property in Spring Green, Wisconsin,
which he worked on in the office of his first employer, Joseph Lyman Silsbee.

This fact is intriguing. Unlike any other founder of Modernism, Wright is known primarily as a residential architect. Though he also designed famous public buildings such as the Guggenheim Museum, the Johnson Wax Company headquarters, and Unity Temple, he is primarily recognized for his contributions to the evolution of the progressive house responding to new social patterns and contemporary structural systems: the Robie House, Hollyhock House, Fallingwater, the Usonian houses.

Yet throughout his career Wright thought about the city. It was a theme that grew with time; we can trace the gradual evolution of his ideas about the city as a design problem, as he experienced revelations, proposed far-sighted solutions, and built his iconoclastic, jarring, influential designs right there in the center of the public square. He designed or built banks, hotels, churches, offices, motels, colleges, retail stores, factories, civic centers, theaters, medical clinics, schools, and even car dealerships and gas stations. Beyond those are his unbuilt conceptual designs for cinemas, tourist attractions, skyscrapers, resorts, laundries, funeral homes, state capitols, opera houses, and

a host of other building types. Together with his residential designs, these flesh out his vision of an entire city.

He thought about the city as imaginatively as—and in ways more accurately than—most other Modern architects. He was, after all, the first major Modern architect to think seriously and creatively about suburbia, the inevitable multi-centered extension of the existing centralized city. He thought not only about individual buildings in the suburbs, but how they would relate to each other to create a thriving, healthy metropolitan life.

Whether he was designing a house or a city, Wright saw architecture as a social art. Even though he used modern structural and building systems whenever possible, the primary purpose of architecture was to create places for people to interact with each other, and with nature. Houses were intriguingly complex configurations of social, structural, and natural elements that inspired his creativity. The 1907 home for the wealthy couple Avery and Queene Coonley was an estate with a grand main house, outlying cottages for gardeners and servants, gardens, workshops, and a school—a community in miniature. But even smaller houses were much more than mere shelter from the elements; they also reflected the relationships of residents. Over the seventy-five years of his career, one of the major

shifts in his designs can be traced to the dramatic changes in the American middle-class family, from the formal Victorian household of society wives, servants, gas lamps, and carriages, to a free-form mix of servantless families, informal suburban life, electricity, and automobiles.

Wright's architecture explored social expression in his singular, artful manner. The exquisite intersection between human life, modern engineering, and nature was arguably the rich protean mix that fundamentally inspired him. This was true whether the design was for a single-family home or an entire city. We are right to honor Wright for his contributions to the private realm of residential architecture. But these same considerations are also the inspiration for his public buildings—fewer in number, but equal in innovation.

For example, none of his public buildings is more jarring nor invigorating than New York's Guggenheim Museum. Its counter-intuitive spiral curves, flexing their muscles, burst all physical and conceptual conventions about what a city looks like. Where Manhattan is static and vertical, the Guggenheim seems to be revolving slowly in its own orbit. When the observer looks up Fifth Avenue toward it, its broad spiral bands seem to be moving outward, horizontally, over the street toward Central Park—the only other Manhattan artifact that shares its kinship with

Opposite and previous pages 6–7: Unity Chapel, Taliesin North, Spring Green, Wisconsin, 1886.

Above and below: Unity Chapel, Taliesin North, 1886. Designed while a teenaged Wright worked with architect Joseph Lyman Silsbee in Chicago, this small family chapel was conceived and executed in the fashionable Shingle Style.

Nature. The Guggenheim has more in common with the lakes and bosks of Frederick Law Olmsted's design than with the pointy-topped or squared-off skyscrapers, which Wright considered "glass prisons" creating "unhealthy canyons."[1] The Guggenheim is not only his rebuke of that misbegotten metropolis, but also his emphatic enunciation of the qualities of a true city.

As his career progressed, we can see Wright's dawning awareness that each individual house he built was part of a larger system of human habitation and economy—the public space. Each house was complete in itself, but he also became increasingly aware of its civic context as well as its natural setting. His designs for public buildings allowed him to expand on those ideas. The ultimate result was his ideal city, Broadacre City. It was in many

ways the idealized theoretical prototype of the great suburban metropolises that would develop in the United States through the twentieth century.

Most of Wright's designs, especially after 1930, can be seen as his Promethean crusade to build Broadacre City, one building at a time.

THE PUBLIC PRAIRIE

Most of Wright's houses through the Prairie years, in the first decade of the century, were constructed in the relatively new suburbs, an increasingly significant segment of thriving cities like Chicago, his hometown. These houses and their drives, lawns, carriage houses, and garages acknowledged their connection to a larger landscape of streetcars and town centers outside the Loop, and a social order that allowed the middle class to live in closer contact with natural settings.

A variety of commissions arriving in his office allowed Wright to begin to sketch out how his essential ideas applied to facets of the suburban city other than residences, including social clubs, banks, office buildings, hotels, entertainment centers, country clubs, factories, art galleries, shops, and schools. True to his idea of Organic Architecture—that a design should grow out of a building's purpose and function as well as its structure and materials, "the integrity of innate structure"—each of these had a distinct form.[2] Each was a strand in a strong urban fabric.

Wright's residential designs in this period were superlative; at the same time he developed a parallel set of public forms, a Prairie Style for commercial and civic buildings. Other Prairie architects, including William Gray Purcell, George Elmslie, George Maher, Dwight Perkins, Barry Byrne, and Walter Burley Griffin—as well as Louis Sullivan himself—joined him in this exploration, and built many more examples of banks, courthouses, office buildings, schools, and churches than did Wright throughout the Midwest.

Handsome, symmetrical, clean-lined, these brick or stone structures had a solid, forceful, and contemporary presence on their streets. Wright's 1905 Smith Bank in Dwight, Illinois, is typical. In his Prairie houses, Wright expressed the wood or brick structural frame on their facades; in this one-story bank, the stone structure is expressed across the facade with stone posts and lintels framing deep-set windows. Its entry is foursquare, elaborated by stone pylons and delicate light standards.

In other commercial or civic buildings, Wright borrowed more directly from the residential vocabulary he had developed. The 1906 Pettit Memorial Chapel (for a funeral home) and the 1905 E. W. Cummings Real Estate Office (now demolished) are variations on the low, residentially scaled country clubs and houses Wright designed for suburban areas.

Wright's public buildings played a substantial role in the establishment of abstraction in the aesthetic of Modern architecture; these designs used the inherent beauty and presence of their materials to establish their monumentality in the city. The plain walls of brick or concrete at the Abraham Lincoln Center, Unity Temple, and Larkin Building would lead to the stark glass walls of the iconic Modern Seagram Building by Ludwig Mies van der Rohe and Philip Johnson a half-century later. The 1903 Abraham Lincoln Center, for example, was a six-story social center, as finely chiseled and immaculately proportioned as any design by Wright's mentor, Louis Sullivan. It had been a contentious design and construction; the client was the Rev. Jenkin Lloyd Jones, an uncle of Wright's and as certain and hardheaded as any in the clan.

Above and below: Unity Chapel, Taliesin North, 1886. Wright was laid to rest in 1959 in the chapel's family graveyard, as were his children.

The Lincoln Center makes a strong pairing with the 1903 Larkin Building in Buffalo, New York. It was a thoroughly modern building type: an office headquarters for a mail-order business bringing the advanced goods of national life to isolated farmers and small towns across the nation with the aid of a modern distribution system of trains, roads, telegraph, and telephone. The project emerged from a residential commission; William Martin, for whom Wright designed a house in 1902, was the brother of Darwin D. Martin, an executive of the Larkin Company (and later a Wright residential client). Wright reconceived the idea of office space as a five-story cathedral of commerce. Most employees were seated on the main floor (at Wright-designed work stations) beneath a tall well topped by a skylight. Balconies looked down on the busy scene; inspiring sculptures and carved words adorned the walls inside and out. Modern air conditioning

transformed the hot, sweaty summers into astounding comfort—and productivity. Set in an industrial district—not in the center of downtown—the building was akin to the sprawling suburban factories seen fifty years later, though rendered as a set of clean brick forms with strong corner pylons and secondary horizontal insets marking each floor—a larger version of the commercial Prairie aesthetic.

These confident and original designs mark the evolution of Wright's thinking about the civic presence of public buildings. They culminated with a 1904 suburban church, Unity Temple in Oak Park, Illinois, one of his greatest public buildings. It was intimately connected to the family life and progressive design of the suburban houses he was building nearby. The design grew from a compelling mix of challenges perfectly tailored to inspire the dynamic, driven young designer to an astonishing solution. First, it was to be his most

prominent public building—in the center of his hometown. Second, it was to be constructed of concrete, one of the malleable, exciting materials of the age guaranteed to stimulate new forms and new possibilities. Third, it was a religious building intended to embody an idealistic spiritual symbolism.

He put his all into the design. The concrete construction inspired sharp-edged planes arranged vertically and horizontally in a rhythmic composition of solids and voids, subtle insets and shadow lines. Upright pylons firmly anchored the corners, while layers of flat slabs capped the roofs.

Inside, the chaste Unitarian philosophy led to a religious space utterly devoid of overt symbols or traditional iconography, a space where light poured in from the entire ceiling through a grid of skylights. The balconies, podium, and ceilings were knitted together by lines of wood trim ornament into a single three-

Opposite and below: Abraham Lincoln Center, Chicago, Illinois, 1903.
Right: Larkin Company Administration Building, Buffalo, New York, 1903.
Though his residential designs established his fame, Wright was always interested in the design of public buildings.
Drawing of Frank Lloyd Wright is Copyright © 2008 The Frank Lloyd Wright Foundation, Taliesin West, Scottsdale, AZ.

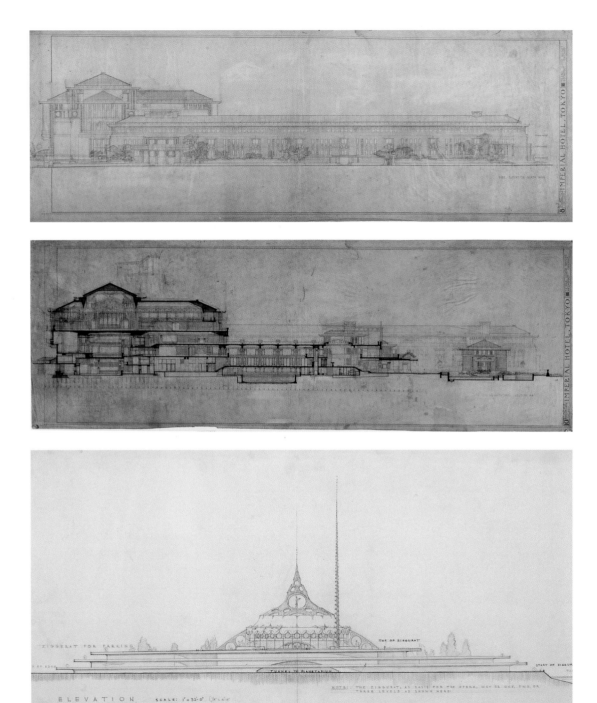

dimensional unity with energetic variety. Owing nothing to traditional architecture, and filled with originality, this opulent abstraction would be one of the keystones of the wide-ranging Modern revolution of the twentieth century.

Despite these forays into abstraction, Wright also continued to insist on the value of ornament. He never lost his love of amplification, of working out his underlying themes and forms in ever more intricate detail and decoration. The contrast of plain and intricate gave scale to a structure, and provided a human warmth and appeal to the eye that Wright would always use, whether it was the cast concrete block of the Ennis House, rugged desert stone walls at Taliesin West, or anodized gold balls along the fascias at Marin County Civic Center. Wright would later be criticized for this ornamentalism; it placed him squarely at odds with the minimalist mainstream of the 1950s. It could be seen as clearly in the 1915 Imperial Hotel—considered one of his masterpieces—as in the 1958 Baghdad Opera House, a late design which most critics have considered self-indulgent and "kitschy," and evidence that he was past his prime.[3] But where others considered it exaggeration or undisciplined excess, Wright called it "exuberance" as William Blake defined the term: the "fullness of the expression of nature."[4] "Liberty is not license, exaggeration is not exuberance," Wright proclaimed.[5]

Though for other founding Modernists, a lack of ornament was a proud badge of their rejection of historicism, Wright considered such ornament essential. The 1909 City National Bank

Left, top and middle: Imperial Hotel, Tokyo, Japan, 1915.
Left, bottom: Opera House, Baghdad, Iraq, 1957.
Opposite: Midway Gardens, Chicago, Illinois, 1913.
These multi-use complexes in urban settings drew out Wright's fertile creativity.

Drawings of Frank Lloyd Wright are Copyright © 2008 The Frank Lloyd Wright Foundation, Taliesin West, Scottsdale, AZ.

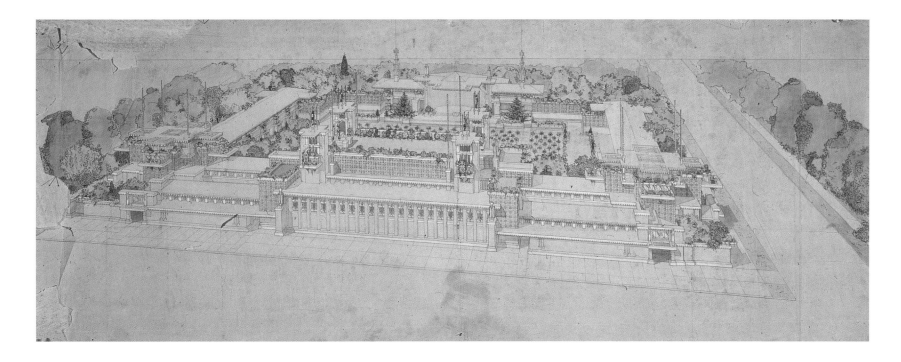

building in Mason City, Iowa, establishes a strong structural system of brick piers, but then ornaments each column capital with an organic flourish—as had Louis Sullivan, and Wright himself in the early Heller and Husser houses. They were like the delicate leaves of a tree crowning the solid trunk. This Modern ornamentalism strengthened after 1915 in Wright's Midway Gardens, in the Imperial Hotel, in the A. D. German Warehouse, and in the textile block houses of Los Angeles.

By 1910 Wright's restless imagination was ready to move beyond the series of single family houses pouring into his office; his growing urbanist sense moved toward carefully considered collections of homes, from the loosely connected Ravine Bluffs, to the more closely structured Quadruple Block homes (unbuilt) of 1913. But his Midway Gardens (1913) in Chicago and then the magnificent Imperial Hotel in Tokyo (1915–1921) offered opportunities to apply his ideas to large, complex, and definitively public buildings. In Midway Gardens the intricate program of restaurants, theaters,

kitchens, signage, intimate enclosed areas, and open-air terraces were mated with a remarkable original ornamental motif that extended from building to signs to furniture and decorative elements. The Imperial Hotel was as sprawling and complex for its day as today's Las Vegas hotels, a miniature city handling hundreds of visitors, guests, revelers, workers, officials, and the general public in one fluid space. As interested as Wright was in expressing modern structural systems, he was even more interested in the human dimension of architecture: the creation of social spaces for modern people.

Clearly, major commissions such as Midway Gardens and the Imperial Hotel ignited his talents. They also held the promise of a thriving and influential architecture practice to fulfill his ambitions as well as his ego. Shortly after, another large and multi-faceted project came along with client Aline Barnsdall: an artistic community in the new city of Los Angeles, to include a legitimate theater, a movie theater, shops, housing, school, and a magnificent home for parties, political gatherings, and

performances on top of Olive Hill in east Hollywood. These larger projects embodied the complexity of modern social interactions that were of great interest to Wright. His long-suffering tolerance of the strong-willed Barnsdall, one of the most difficult clients of his career, may be partially explained by the intriguing nature of the project she brought to him.

But that thriving practice was not to be. His son, Lloyd Wright, blamed his father's long absences in Japan for the decay of his client base and national reputation—essential elements for an ongoing architecture practice. There were the scandals of his personal life (the sensational death of his mistress in a fire at his Wisconsin home, Taliesin, in 1914, his tumultuous marriage to Miriam Noel before his shocking dalliance with Olgivanna Lazovich), though profligate lifestyles were not necessarily negative publicity in the artistic world. Lloyd probably came closest to the truth; as dynamic as Wright had seemed in 1910, he had fallen out of touch with clients and fashion by 1920. Of his two showpiece public works, Midway Gardens

was soon put out of business by Prohibition, and the Imperial Hotel was half a world away from Chicago. Struggling for work after its completion, Wright retreated to Taliesin to wait out a fifteen year professional drought.

REBUILDING

This period was hardly a creative drought, though. Besides exploring new structural systems (textile concrete block construction for the Freeman,

Opposite and above: Imperial Hotel, Tokyo, 1915. For the large public buildings he designed, Wright developed a civic architecture distinct from, but as highly evolved as, the Prairie house designs of the same era.

Photographs are Courtesy The Frank Lloyd Wright Foundation, Taliesin West, Scottsdale, AZ.

Storer, Millard, Ennis, and Lloyd Jones houses) and new topographies (dry, hilly Southern California) during the 1920s, he continued to think about how individual buildings fitted together into a larger city. He turned his attention to fresh designs based on his Organic philosophy for a range of buildings that constitute a city. Each house, church, skyscraper, or automobile objective was fully realized in itself as a design, but also served a role as part of an entire city— and a living society. These ideas would coalesce in 1935 as a model of Broadacre City, but before that he explored and evolved a dozen different building types: resort cabins and barges at Lake Tahoe; subdivisions and resorts in the Hollywood Hills and Chandler, Arizona; and churches, theaters, country clubs, and schools.

Already he was taking note of the automobile's influence on living patterns and architecture. The car permitted a new rhythm and scale to the city about which Wright was

enthusiastic. His willingness to accept the automobile, as a twentieth century technology (just like steel, concrete, and plate glass), set him apart from many other architects who either rejected it or felt awkward designing for its demands for space, storage, and turning radii. "See the extended highway as one great horizontal line of Usonian freedom expanding life consistently everywhere," he would later write.[6] Early on he saw the impact of car travel on the arrangement of buildings in the city and the countryside, heralding a new kind of suburban metropolis. The unbuilt 1925 Gordon Strong Automobile Objective and Planetarium in the Maryland countryside accepted the willingness of people to get in their new cars and see the country; its distinctive spiral form was dictated by the turning radius of a car, which Wright exploited in a vivid conic pyramidal form.

Wright looked as carefully at skyscrapers, the essence of the modern city. He had, of course, been Louis Sullivan's right-hand man during the design of some of his mentor's most brilliant and seminal skyscraper buildings, including the 1890 Wainwright Building. Wright's Luxfer Prism Company building design—an eleven-story building that qualified as a skyscraper in 1895 (the 1894 Reliance Building by Burnham and Root was sixteen stories)—was an exercise in inventing a square, glass-filled window to bring light deep into the floor plate, in the tradition of the Chicago window used by Sullivan, Burnham and Root, and others. During his Prairie period in 1912, he applied the Prairie vocabulary to a twenty-three-story skyscraper design, the Press Building in San Francisco, a simple vertical slab capped by a wide flat eave. The 1924 National Life Insurance Company skyscraper for Chicago was a very different design of thirty-two stories; moving away from the solid rectilinear compositions of the Larkin and Press Buildings of his early years, Wright boldly adapted the frame's potential to support a lightweight glass exterior—a curtain wall in a sense—to create a jagged, multi-winged, crystalline tower. It was clear evidence that Wright was not stuck in the past, as many of his critics imagined.

The 1921 St. Mark's in the Bouwerie skyscraper can be seen as Wright's alternative to the submissions to the 1921 Chicago Tribune Tower competition, one of the most influential explorations of potential skyscraper designs; proudly, Wright himself never entered competitions.[7] Though never built, Eliel

Above and right: Arizona Biltmore, Phoenix, Arizona, 1927. Albert McArthur, a former employee of Wright, was the architect of the Biltmore, with Wright as the influential consultant. The luxurious resort used his textile block concrete structural system. Its massing, public spaces, and ornament constitute a distinct Organic public architecture based on Wright's concepts.

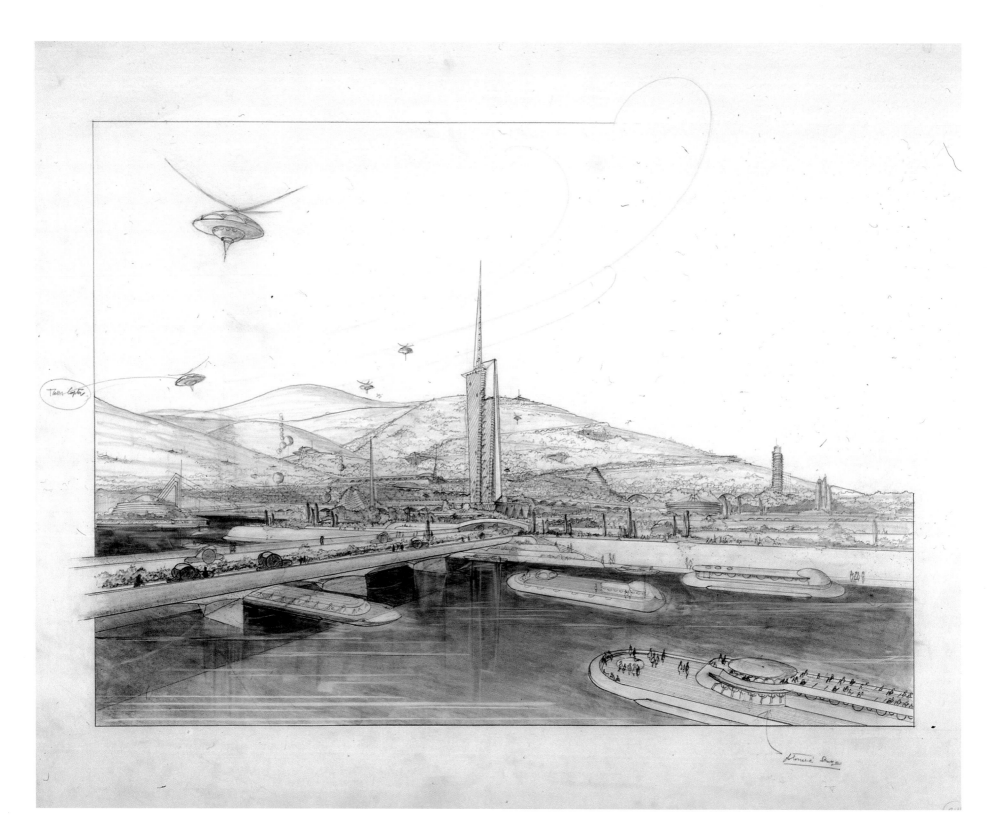

Saarinen's first-prize-winning tower, a stone-clad cliff with sleek vertical lines and well-proportioned setbacks reaching to the sky, was so arresting that it influenced a generation of skyscrapers. But its modernity pales in comparison to Wright's St. Mark's apartment tower. As was his habit, he recycled this solution as a collection of towers in the 1940 Crystal Heights Hotel for Washington D.C. In the final version of the design, built in 1955 as the Price Tower in Bartlesville, Oklahoma, offices and apartments were interwoven, giving the lightweight metal and glass exterior a jazzy, contrapuntal energy. It was the only true skyscraper he was able to build.

Three things are striking about the designs Wright developed during the 1920s. First, the variety and freshness of the solutions are astonishing. Second, they show how his thought was moving toward the design of every facet of a city. They imply a city of tremendous expressive variety, where each design was drawn from a function or site. Third, they embraced the newest trends in materials, social lifestyles, and technology of the twentieth century.

BROADACRES

By 1930 Wright had reconstituted his own life, personally and (to an extent) professionally. He had remarried, to Olgivanna Lazovich, in 1928. They had jointly set up the Taliesin Fellowship in 1933 as an artistic community revolving around and supporting his work. Spring Green's Taliesin became a small self-sufficient town in itself; he added work, office, and residential space for the apprentices who came to study under him and live together in an idealistic community. He built farm buildings and roads, and bought neighboring farms as satellites. It was, for Wright, an ideal rural community that replicated the elements of a social city: architectural work went on daily, musical performances, lectures, and movies were staged weekly, the maintenance and

husbandry of a farm and crops were regular work for all. Picnics were regular relaxations.

Taliesin represented a highly sophisticated culture in the middle of the bucolic countryside—a Wrightian ideal. The city and society did not—should not—have to be cut off from nature, he believed. Farming, the beauty of meadows and trees, the normal presence of animals and agriculture for food—all the cycles, awareness, and dependencies of humankind on nature were absolutely essential to the health of a city and of society itself, Wright believed. The philosophy seen at Taliesin was translated on a much larger scale to the ideal city of Broadacres. It had been forming in his thought for years; now, with a workforce of apprentices, he designed a large model of this futuristic city, which he displayed in museums, department stores, and empty storefronts everywhere and anywhere he could. With the renewed international attention given his work upon the completion of Fallingwater, the Johnson Wax building, and the first Usonian house in 1936, professional and public curiosity about this utopian city grew.

It is essential to understand Broadacre City if we are to fairly evaluate Wright's public architecture. Each building he designed (especially after 1935) was, in effect, a fragment of Broadacre City realized; beyond their client's needs and their structure's demands, these designs responded to a broad social vision. In a 1945 book, *When Democracy Builds* (and the 1958 revision *The Living City*) Wright presented his jeremiad against the existing city, and his revelation of a heavenly city. It is written with prophetic certainty. As a piece of writing it swings between pontifications in Wright's clipped, outrageously self-assured style of speech, and passages whose curt assertions are nearly unreadable. His public buildings did not fit into the conceptual framework of the capitalist, credit-fueled city societies that were the norm in America—and which he detested philosophically. This is one reason why his designs were and are

Above: Press Building, San Francisco, California, 1912.
Opposite: Broadacre City, 1958.
As an early Wright design for a skyscraper, the Press Building uses rectilinear geometries similar to the Larkin Building and Unity Temple. The later Broadacre City drawing shows some of the complex geometrical forms Wright explored as his career developed. The drawing illustrates the horizontal suburban metropolis urban form that he advocated, punctuated by landmark, freestanding skyscrapers.

Drawings of Frank Lloyd Wright are Copyright © 2008 The Frank Lloyd Wright Foundation, Taliesin West, Scottsdale, AZ.

challenging. At heart Wright proposed not only a new public architecture, but also a new (or reformed) society. He followed the ideals of the solid farmers of Thomas Jefferson's America, a decentralized agrarian society that began to die out in the early nineteenth century as Alexander Hamilton's centralized cities of trade, manufacturing, and credit gained a solid foothold.

Society, technology, nature—each demanded a fresh response. The economic structure of Broadacre City was as radically unconventional as the architecture that expressed it. Ever the iconoclast, Wright also spoke forthrightly about the salvation that the automobile brought to the modern city. Many critics since have noted similarities between

Broadacre City and the modern car-oriented suburban metropolises that were actually built around every American city after World War II. Though this comparison is often cast negatively, Wright presents the philosophical underpinnings of this decentralized city—while he would have objected to the continuing influence of landlords and bankers in today's suburban metropolises. But the philosophy of Broadacres also speaks about a city living in tune with the ecological balance of nature, themes that became major cultural trends after Wright's death in 1959.

Wright presented his ideal modern city as being, at its core, an expression of the ancient character of humankind as wandering tribes, nomads living in forests and meadows. Modern

man also belonged near "the good ground," he asserted.[8] The automobile permitted this lifestyle in keeping with modern technology.

In contrast, the problem with existing cities, by Wright's analysis, was that they evolved from the ancient cave dwellers—arch-conservatives who sought safety and protection above all; they would give up their liberty to band together in increasingly congested cities under a controlling feudal economic elite. He traced the city's ugliness and failure to the cardinal sins of centralization, speculators, and "landlords, machine-lords, and money-lords."[9] They built walls and fortresses, manifested in the iconic modern image of Manhattan's clustered skyscrapers.

Wright's new city would be built by—and hasten the spread of—a New Man. This broad creative society relied on such classes as Artist Agrarian, Artist Mechanic, Inspired Teacher, Inventor, and Scientist.[10] Free in thought, with free choice, free of old rent-based economic systems, the New Man would discover and nurture his true nature—and the architecture and art that expressed it (i.e., Organic architecture.) The "ghastly" efficiencies of capitalism and centralization (seen in traditional cities) did not justify the costly burden of materialism that beat down man's spirit.[11]

Though it has the ring of myth, Wright's narrative of nomads and cave dwellers is manifested in very specific architectural and urban forms. The modern cave dwellers lived in the literal fortress-caves of skyscrapers; the modern nomads lived in Broadacre City.

And so Wright's civic thinking, as it matured in the 1930s, proposed a multitude of systemic reforms for banking, religion, agriculture,

Above and opposite: Frank L. Smith Bank, Dwight, Illinois, 1905.
This confident design shows how Wright adapted the modern, structurally expressive concepts of the Prairie houses to a public building.

government, the arts, and business. These were the foundation for a healthy city, he believed. And his architecture, growing organically out of these ideas, and the very shape of the city itself, would both express and support this reformed society.

There was to be no central downtown to Broadacres; business, governmental offices, sports facilities, markets, churches, museums, and all the other necessities of a thriving city were spread throughout the decentralized city. "Centralization has built (but never designed)" and has warped the human spirit into a "sidewalk happy" citizen who has "traded his origins and native pastimes with streams, woods, fields, and animals...The mechanical screech turns citified heads like a songbird," he angrily protested.[12] Schools were nothing but "knowledge-factories"; skyscrapers were nothing but "the gravestone of capitalistic centralization."[13]

The centralization of men and capital was no longer "wise or human."[14] Wright preferred the moral tradition of nomadic hunter-warriors, "bred under the stars" and relying on "mobility for safety."[15] Though 1958 was only the dawn of the age of space travel, intercontinental ballistic missiles, and the Internet, Wright realized that the ancient mentality of the walled fort was outmoded. Modern science dictated a modern life with light, space, and freedom of movement—a "command of time and distance,"—which were the qualities at the heart of the Broadacre City's concept.[16] Essential to this arrangement was the automobile, which permitted "a new sense of spacing based upon speed."[17] Cars would lead inevitably to a new and better culture.

Left and opposite: City National Bank and Park Inn Hotel, Mason City, Iowa, 1909.
The strongly emphasized foundation piers and colorful ornament complement each other. This handsome structure includes a bank, offices, hotel, and shops. Tall pilasters above the ground floor create a modern rhythm and scale for this Midwestern city.

As hazy as some of this economic theory sounds, it was inspiration for specific architectural and planning ideas that Wright felt intuitively—and which cannot be easily discounted. The spacing and rhythm of Broadacre City was a well-considered alternative to the crowded, high-density cities of skyscrapers, congestion, factories, and concrete; function and livability, not property values, should dictate the proper placement and relationship of such towers. Wright also redesigned nearly every other type of building to be included in this ideal city also:

Farm Architecture

At Broadacre's heart was a citizenry who lived on the land. Single-family houses sat on a minimum of one acre, which allowed each family to raise its own food; surplus could be sold at small farmers markets that also served as community centers around the city. The distinction between urban and rural was purposely blurred.

Wright had begun to design farm buildings at his own home in Wisconsin in 1911. They went far beyond simple utility. They are part of nature, part of the clustered spires of trees, part of the rolling land and the rock outcroppings. He wished to unite nature and mankind at their most intimate point of contact: the production of food, essential to life, from the soil, seed, and rain. In a large populous city, that required the intervention of humans to organize, nurture, reap and distribute food. Humans worked with nature to produce food. His designs for his own farm buildings honor the color, the complexity, the geometry of nature. And so did the design of farm buildings which were the basic social unit of Broadacre City. One prototype house included a farmyard, stalls, and other outbuildings along with the home as part of a unified compound. Another was a two-story design of considerable sophistication—it was, in fact, the first design for the 1933 Willey House.

These farm homesteads alone, spreading spaciously over the landscape, dictated a low-

rise city. This bestowed two important benefits: citizens were liberated from the crowded cities, and they were put back in touch with nature, the ancestral habitat of the human race. Since the 1930s many architects and urban planners criticized the crime, congestion, and disorganization of most cities; Wright agreed. But where Victor Gruen, a widely influential architect-planner, proposed to increase density by double-decking urban streets to divide service vehicles and trucks from cars and pedestrians, Wright sought to diffuse density. Broadacre was a clear and sensible alternative.

Factory Architecture

The factory was also a part of Broadacre City.

Wright had designed several throughout his career: the E-Z Polish factory in Chicago for the Darwin brothers, for whom he designed noteworthy houses; the Johnson Wax building added research laboratories in 1944. The 1955 design for the Lenkurt Company in Menlo Park, California, would have been an early and distinguished model for the nascent Silicon Valley. The broad structure used the slender dendriform columns he designed for the Johnson building. Along with architects Edward Durell Stone in his design for Stuart Pharmaceuticals in Pasadena, California, and Eliel and Eero Saarinen for General Motors in Warren, Michigan, Wright subscribed to the idea that the smoky, grimy factory of the early

Industrial Revolution could be replaced with a clean, pleasant, beautiful, well-landscaped factory. It was an essential in Broadacre City.

Church Architecture

From the family chapel in Spring Green to Unity Temple, church architecture had inspired Wright throughout his career. By 1940 he was thinking in terms of a new, changing aesthetic of broader, simple shapes and irregular geometries, seen in the 1940 Kansas City Community Christian Church, and the 1955 Kalita Humphreys Theater in Dallas. They share their asymmetric geometries and juxtaposed volumes with the Guggenheim, designed in the same period. A broad cantilevered porch runs along the second-floor level of the Community Christian Church, emphasizing the strong horizontal lines that Wright had used in the wide eaves of his Prairie houses, and in more abstract form in the jutting balconies of Fallingwater. In the Community Christian Church he uses them in the oblique angles of an irregular site.

The Kansas City Community Christian Church is also a building that turns itself inside out, merging and blurring the line between indoor and outdoor spaces. Of course Modern architecture had long been intrigued by this redefinition of space, once modern structural materials and glass allowed them more flexibility. But where an architect like Richard Neutra (who as a young architect in Vienna revered Wright) simply dissolved the wall by using glass, Wright choose a more spatially complex method of uniting indoors and out. At the church, a broad open stairwell links the lower chapel with the main auditorium level with the second floor office level; but then Wright continues the same spiraling staircase up to the roof level, where he planned a broad terrace and an intricate crown-like steeple, never built. The clear concept of that open stairwell as a spatial link to unite the spacious auditorium, lobby, and roof terrace illustrate Wright's daring spatial exploration.

Due to budget cutbacks during its construction at the beginning of World War II, the building did not have the opportunity to prove itself. Disputes with the client led Wright to disown the project at one point. Its overuse of stucco in the fabrication of ornamental grills that clearly should have been wood does not allow the final building to show its design to the best effect.

Another church, the Unitarian Meeting House, is one of Wright's most widely imitated buildings. Forty years after the Unity Temple in Oak Park, the spirit of Unitarianism inspired him to a very different solution. In 1946 America was about to commence a building boom. The public's relief with the end of war and the hopeful return of prosperity led a large segment of the public to embrace Modern architecture as the look of the future. Even many churches—often the most conservative in terms of architectural form—looked to Modernism for a new expression of spirituality. Architects sought to define that spirit in modern terms, and Wright's simple solution of an A-frame roof proved instantly popular and frequently copied. The overall symbolism was evocative; Wright himself described it as the form of two hands joined in prayer and supplication. But further subtle design choices underscored that aspiration reflected in the form. The A-frame is tilted upward; the main prow thrusts out and up into the air. Inside, the meeting room rose from low-ceilinged areas up to the altar and an expanse of glass as the roof soared upward. The direction and energy of the building swept the petitioner up to something higher.

As if proving his fertile imagination, Wright's other churches built in the last decade of his career also took dramatically different directions. The Annunciation Greek Orthodox Church in Milwaukee, Wisconsin, followed the traditional centrality of the churches of that denomination to create a circular building. The Beth Sholom Synagogue outside Philadelphia, Pennsylvania, gave Wright the chance to return to a design from 1926, the Steel Cathedral for a Million

Above, opposite, and following pages: William H. Pettit Memorial Chapel, Belvidere, Illinois, 1906.
For this funeral chapel in a suburban area, Wright adapted the forms of his suburban Prairie residential architecture. A half century later he would use the same strategy in designing a series of small medical office buildings.

Right, far right, and opposite:
Frank Lloyd Wright Field Office,
San Francisco, California, 1951.
In a small office building in
downtown San Francisco,
Wright designed this interior for
his West Coast office with his
former apprentice Aaron Green.
This interior is now installed at
the Heinz Architectural Center,
Pittsburgh, Pennsylvania.

People, to be built in New York. The imagery blends appropriate images from Jewish history: a great irregular pyramidal roof is tent-like, and it rises like a sacred mountain; it rides on a low-walled bowl foundation that is ark-like. As at Pfeiffer Chapel at Florida Southern College and Unity Temple, the roof is not opaque but spectacularly luminous, sheathed in translucent plastic panels; at night the sacred mountain glows. The 1958 Pilgrim Congregational Church in Redding, California, was to have an addition, never built. Stem-like angular beams are exposed on the exterior, revealing the structure; the roof hangs from these frames. Inside Wright surrounds the congregation with the warm natural stone and wood of his best residential designs. The expressive potential of ecclesiastical architecture suited Wright and his Organic forms as he sought to express

something more than the minimal structuralism that informed mainstream Modern architecture in the mid-twentieth century.

School Architecture

The Ruskinian Wright proposed studios and workshops spread throughout Broadacre City. "Design Centers" would teach young architects. Likewise the city had small schools throughout the city; his design for the 1923 Little Dipper, a handsome school on the brow of Olive Hill for Aline Barnsdall's art colony in Los Angeles, was an early version; a later version, the Wyoming School, was built near his home in Spring Green.

Commercial Architecture

Wright's built commercial architecture was usually designed for small-town streets, or for a suburban, car-oriented site (to be discussed

below). Wright downgraded the prestigious position of the bank from a stone monument (even like his own 1905 Smith Bank) to a more utilitarian structure. For a knowledgeable client like banker Walter Bimson (of the Valley National Bank, Tucson, Arizona), however, he designed a handsome "daylight" bank with a skylighted roof in 1947. Anderton Court shops on Rodeo Drive in Beverly Hills exhibit a dramatic evolution from his 1909 bank, offices, shops, and hotel in Mason City, Iowa. Where that multi-use project continued the flat, brick, three-story scale of the surrounding small-town commercial district, Anderton Court insists on breaking up its facade into angled planes of glass. As at the Kansas City Community Christian Church, a central, jaggedly spiraling ramp is the central circulation system. It places shoppers on display as they wind up the several levels of small shops. This open-air

ramp is also the main feature on the facade, cantilevered over the sidewalk and pinned down with a handsome, quill-like spire of anodized aluminum similar to those used on several contemporary projects, including Marin County Civic Center and the Baghdad Opera House.

Health Care Architecture

Broadacre City's hospitals were to be smaller, more numerous, and homelike. They were not to display the "paraphernalia of abnormality," he wrote.[18] Thus for a series of suburban medical clinics Wright built, he borrowed from his suburban residential design vocabulary. The program was similar: a lobby/waiting room that greeted clients, like a living room; a series of small examination rooms like bedrooms; laboratories like a kitchen. The Meyers and Kundert medical clinics used the Usonian forms

of red brick chimneys linked by a wide-eaved horizontal roof; the Fassbinder Clinic used oblique geometries for a prominent mansard-like roof that fell close to the ground.

ORGANIZING BROADACRES

Wright organized the sprawling Broadacre City around two contrasting features: the vertical skyscraper and the horizontal compound. "Sterile urban verticality" should be replaced with "natural horizontality—true line of human freedom on earth," he commanded.[19] Much of this ideal city was low-rise, with single-family houses wedded to the good earth, which the residents cultivated outside their back doors. But there was also a need for skyscrapers for apartment-dwellers and offices. They were to

be widely separated, like tall trees in an open meadow. Unlike the high-rise apartment towers of Le Corbusier's Plan Voisin (lined up like dominos about to be knocked down), the space between Wright's towers was working farmland, not vague "parkland."

The tree/meadow metaphor served many purposes in Wright's concept of the skyscraper, so different from the conventional approach of crowding them for economic reasons, cheek to jowl, in central business districts. The free-standing skyscraper could provide its residents with magnificent unobstructed views of the surrounding land; its concentrated population could be more easily digested by the surrounding city; the form of a shapely, tapering tower aesthetically provided a counterpoint balance to the horizontal city around it; its architecture could be truly appreciated and admired.

Skyscraper Architecture

As we have seen above, Wright had been designing tall buildings since the 1890s when he worked with Louis Sullivan. Within a dozen years early in the century he had conceived the slab-like Press Building, the crystalline National Life Insurance Building, and the spiky spear of St. Mark's in the Bouwerie. After 1940 he designed several more. The fourteen-story Research Tower for Johnson Wax continued the curved surfaces of brick and glass tubing of the 1936 office building adjacent, but its unusual central structural core—like a tree trunk with the floors cantilevered off in the manner of flat branches—illustrated Wright's continued interest in inventing new structures and giving the distinctive form. The 1946 Rogers Lacy Hotel in Dallas inaugurated yet another solution to the high-rise tower by inverting the intuitive taper (wide at the bottom, narrow at top) into a crystalline stalactite seemingly hanging from the clouds. Fifty-three stories and sheathed in diamond-shaped scales of glass, it was another tour de force of Wrightian imagination; a large open-atrium lobby inside prefigured by twenty years the Hyatt Regency designs of John Portman; these were truly public spaces to adorn the city. The 1956 Golden Beacon Skyscraper for Chicago showed Wright's disdain for the boxy 1956 Seagram Building designed Mies van der Rohe and Philip Johnson which inspired architects the world over to imitation; to underscore his alternative, Wright proposed the 1956 Mile High Skyscraper, Chicago, as an angled stalagmite growing out of the prairie up to a true cloud-piercing needle.

Besides the Johnson Wax Research Tower, the only skyscraper Wright ever built was the

Opposite and above: Frank Lloyd Wright Field Office, San Francisco, California, 1951.
Wright used built-in furniture and diagonal walls of varying transparency to transform a standard rectangular office space.

1952 Price Tower in Bartlesville, Oklahoma, modeled on the St. Mark's in the Bouwerie apartments as a tall and soaring thing. It combines offices and apartments; the delineation of these different interior spaces on the exterior gives the surface variety. The different interlocking pieces, multiplied over twenty floors, slide past each other, one shooting above the next, until they touch the sky in a thin spire. Balconies and kitchen bays jut out as counterpoint. Horizontal louvers provide sunshade. Weathered copper, embossed with organic ornament, echoes the organic metaphor of the tree standing in the meadow. It is a thoroughly modern design in its fresh forms and expressive structure, but it is as far from the

mechanistic Modern imagery of the Seagram Building as can be imagined.

Suburban Complexes

As important to Broadacres' urban character as these skyscrapers were low-rise campuses of related buildings. As Wright's individual buildings depended on the expression of an internal balance of well-articulated elements, in these complexes he brought the same attention to the interrelationships of individual structures to each other.

One of the first of these projects he took on was the design of Aline Barnsdall's Olive Hill art colony in Los Angeles. Though only the main house and two subsidiary houses were built,

Right:
Mile High
Skyscraper,
Chicago,
Illinois, 1956.
Drawing of Frank
Lloyd Wright is
Copyright © 2008
The Frank Lloyd
Wright Foundation,
Taliesin West,
Scottsdale, AZ.

Opposite:
Ocatillo
Desert Camp,
Chandler,
Arizona,
1928. Mr. and
Mrs. Wright
and their
daughters are
shown in
front of their
winter camp
in Arizona.
Wright was
working on
the San
Marcos in the
Desert resort
(never built)
nearby.
Photograph is
Courtesy The Frank
Lloyd Wright
Foundation, Taliesin
West, Scottsdale,
AZ.

the complex was to have included theaters, shops, a cinema, and housing for artists. Their arrangement was fairly simple: the high point of the hill determined the siting of the main house, and the surrounding city streets determined the location of the public theaters and apartments planned. Later, larger projects, including the 1921 Doheny Ranch plan and 1927 San Marcos in the Desert resort, caused Wright to examine the interplay of existing topography and abstract geometry in the effective arrangement of many buildings.

Taliesin West in Scottsdale, Arizona, and Florida Southern College in Lakeland, Florida, illustrate Wright's mature approach to these complex compounds. Both are, in effect, designs for communities: one for an arts community, the other an educational community. Taliesin West is, of course, Wright's own winter home, but as the first building designed specifically to serve the Taliesin Fellowship founded in 1933, it was planned for the support of the community, with offices, drafting rooms, shops, theaters, vaults, suites, dormitories, dining rooms, living rooms, and desert gardens and pools. Florida Southern College was an entire campus, with classrooms, library, chapels, a planetarium, laboratories, and of course gardens and pools. Both are essentially low-rise, spread over the landscape; both deal with extreme climates.

Taliesin West began in 1938 as a desert encampment for his suddenly thriving fellowship. The materials are concrete walls studded with desert rock; their walls rise at a battered angle for stability, and to abstract the shapes of the desert mountains. In vivid contrast, the slanting roof structures are wood or steel and lightweight in comparison to the stony walls. As a winter residence, many of the roofs in the living and drafting areas were originally canvas (later replaced with plastic), which provided a luminous ceiling that balanced the light.

Though the materials are consistent through the compound, the forms of individual buildings are diverse, articulating their purpose for living, working, or gathering. Tying them together are the spaces between the buildings: walkways, trellises, pools or splashing water, sunken patios, laid out along a triangular plan that emphasizes the gently sloping topography, the main buildings, and the approach to them. The spaces flow according to use, from public to private, from outside to inside, from work to play, from collective to individual. Here the irregular angled geometries of the Kansas City Community Christian Church (in contrast to the curving geometries of Johnson Wax and the Guggenheim Museum) find perhaps their fullest expression in three-dimensional spaces defined by an opulent manifestation of natural materials and textures: rocky stone, exposed wood, luxuriant fabrics. It is an entire universe of shapes defining public or collective uses. They create intimacy when necessary, unity when desired; their shapes shift and change as needed, yet create a unified whole throughout the complex.

Florida Southern College uses the same concept (and many of the same angular geometries) as Taliesin West. Like Taliesin West (and in keeping with Wright's tendency to draw close to the earth) the buildings spread over the landscape, connected by long marquees for shade in the hot Florida sun. The architectural scale is maintained here, however, by the overscaled, asymmetrical pylons that hold the thin roof. Their diagonal, ornamented motifs are continued in the main buildings, which punctuate this horizontal campus: Pfeiffer Chapel capped by a skylight; the planetarium as a contrasting, solid, rectangular composition; the semicircular library.

EXURBAN ARCHITECTURE

There are holes in Wright's urban-economic concepts, but it should be noted that he was—unlike most other urban theorists of the time—creative and positive about the potential for the automobile for a livable city. He thereby opened his thinking to many workable ideas appropriate to the new suburban metropolises evolving in Houston, Phoenix, Los Angeles, and elsewhere in the twentieth century—while most critics simply ignored their reality. By denying the auto's positive potential, they removed themselves from meaningful involvement in the development of one of the major trends of twentieth-century urbanism. Wright demonstrated how, through design, the architecture of suburbia could foster a genuine, well-rounded, and satisfying urbanism.

Automobiles and highways allowed this new city to take form in what Wright was calling "exurban" areas.[20] Wright's contribution to the architecture of the automobile—the key to modern suburbia—is controversial today. At times he was a true prophet and master salesman; at other times his designs were either too far ahead of his times, or ignored some essential populist truth about how people liked to live with the car. Still, the automobile was a progressive step beyond the "unwholesome subways" and streetcars of existing cities that should be replaced with buses on flexible routes, he advised.[21] As one of the earliest and greatest suburban architects, Wright had easily accepted the role of the porte-cochere as a Prairie house's entry, and the presence and convenience of the garage. In the Usonian house designs after 1936, the carport was an essential and integrally designed part of the house's public face to the street; the car itself was literally integrated into the architecture as ornament and function.

In the 1920s, the Strong Automobile Objective demonstrated Wright's broad grasp of the automobile's impact on the regional landscape and America's emerging tourist economy. He had also designed vacation houseboats for Lake Tahoe in the 1920s; he proposed inflatable camping cabins in the 1950s. Extrapolating vehicular technology (and the Indian Tours in twelve-cylinder Cadillacs that drove Southwestern tourists to the pueblos of

Arizona and New Mexico in the 1920s), he proposed "mobile hotels" like buses that would drive to scenic areas. Motels also would be luxurious short-term residences in beautiful natural settings. The 1955 Wieland Motor Hotel, in Hagerstown, Maryland, was a two-story design that included circular structures embracing a central grassy terrace with pool and fountain. Another design for the 1956 Bramlett Motor Hotel was a collection of three circular nine-story towers.

It is difficult to imagine the other influential founders of Modernism (Mies van der Rohe, Le Corbusier, or Walter Gropius) being seriously aware of—let alone designing for—America's tourist culture. Unlike them, Wright experienced the American roadside firsthand. Since the 1920s, he and Mrs. Wright drove in their Lincoln Zephyr, Cord, or Lincoln Continental twice yearly between their homes in Wisconsin and Arizona. While he saw much that he disliked and wished to change ("sordid" billboards, poles, and wires, snow fences, air pollution), he also took careful note of practical and populist trends that

represented a new underlying order that architects must understand and use.[22] Of markets he said, "Even if neglected and despised, they are fingers pointing the end of centralism....They are already expanding in the great Southwest."[23] Service stations were a means of general distribution as significant to the decentralized city as the great downtown department stores had been fifty years before. He acknowledged outdoor advertising as a "characteristic art" of the times, and sought to design signs well as an integral part of his architecture; his 1956 gas station included a handsome if under-scaled rooftop sign integrated with the architecture.[24]

As suburbia spread, the need for car-accessible buildings proliferated, and Wright designed drive-in projects including the Adelman drive-in laundry, the 1947 Valley National Bank in Tucson, a roadside market, and the 1948 Daphne funeral home with drive-in facilities. Needless to say, Wright did not invent the drive-in; that was a product of the pragmatic vernacular genius of new cities like Los Angeles. But he clearly

saw the potential for these car-oriented buildings in terms of form and planning—and their potential for coming together in a new kind of suburban city.

The rationalization and beautification of road infrastructure interested him, too. He designed highway grade separations that would allow traffic to flow unimpeded at major intersections. He designed a sinuous concrete crossing for the San Mateo Bridge over San Francisco Bay, and a garage for his civic center project in Pittsburgh. He advocated burying electric wires, and planting trees and flowers along the roadsides.

At a time when many architects and planners downplayed the significance of suburban growth, Wright was at the forefront. He grasped that the landscape of cities and highways could and would be fundamentally altered by the automobile, and he welcomed the change. The living city was not, for Wright, a rehabilitation of the traditional nineteenth-century industrial city, nor a romantic re-creation of any historic models. It was an entire re-imagining of the city. Only when the new city was built would he turn to heal the "cancerous...overgrowth" of the old urban districts.[25]

For all his enthusiasm for the new automobile city, however, Wright built only two public projects for the roadside. They were on opposite ends of the scale: one a gas station in Minnesota, the other a civic center for Marin County, California, designed as a public monument for the highway.

The R. W. Lindholm Service Station is more a didactic building than a fully realized architectural concept. Along with markets,

Left: Annunciation Greek Orthodox Church, Milwaukee, Wisconsin, 1956.
Like Marin County Civic Center and his plan for Baghdad, Wright often used circular geometries in his later public buildings. They created startlingly unconventional architecture that remains controversial.

motels, and art galleries, Wright firmly believed that gas stations could be beautiful if the architect understood their function sufficiently to translate them into an architectural space and structure. In the case of the gas station, he desired to improve the standard prototype by eliminating columns that cars might bump into; pragmatically he covers the service area with a cantilevered roof; gas hoses were to be suspended from above. Besides an office at ground level, he puts one a level above to increase the manager's ability to survey the site. Three service bays extend to one side. And to announce the product, he turns a tall pylon on top of the roof into an Organic ornamental sign.

The architecture's glass and copper materials are boldly faceted and ornamented. He saw the potential of this utilitarian architecture to become a piece of social architecture, as a roadside rest stop designed with shade and services for the comfort of travelers. But for all his enthusiasm for the new car culture, Wright's building fails to fully analyze the problem. The successful 1937 prototype gas station for Texaco Oil by industrial designer Walter Dorwin Teague, for example, used the Streamline Moderne to create a bold, highly visible piece of roadside architecture. The exotic, delicately scaled Organic decorative elements used by Wright lack the bold scale required for a building to "read" in the clutter of the roadside. The "Phillips 66" lettered on the needle pylon is unreadable from afar. Even with a gabled form to the roof, the design is too spindly to have an impact on the eye on the commercial strip. Like Mies van der Rohe—another great Modernist—who designed a weak Hi-Way restaurant in 1948, Wright failed to grasp the balance of image and form, or readability and memorability that the public landscape of the automobile demanded.

Ironically, Wright did in fact have a major impact on the design of the suburban commercial strip in the 1940s and 1950s, but through the influence of his ideas on others. His apprentice John Lautner designed several

roadside restaurants in Los Angeles, including the iconic Henry's and Googies, which helped to establish Modern design as the appropriate aesthetic for the post-war commercial boom. Both used Wright's ideas by taking this new kind of architecture seriously, and by rethinking the problem to develop a successful solution. So startlingly successful was Googies that it gave its name to an entire type of ultramodern roadside architecture. Other Wright admirers, the firm of Armét and Davis, developed a series of coffee shops using Organic design contrasting natural stone or brick walls with sweeping cantilevered roofs, thus combining nature and technology in a definitively Wrightian manner. These younger architects were able to shake off the Victorian fussiness that often overtook Wright to make clear, bold, and meaningful solutions to the problem.

THE CITY DENOUNCED

Wright's visceral disdain for the credit-oriented, royalist impulses of the traditional city made it impossible for him to design anything in its image. The two buildings he built in the very center of such cities are therefore interesting essays in negative architecture—that is, architecture which by its form denounced the very context in which it stood. They are the Guggenheim Museum, and the V. C. Morris Gift Shop.

The Guggenheim Museum is his most assertive denunciation of that decadent city, as blunt and unapologetic an indictment of a society as any prophet could ever pronounce—but still asserting his impulses to seek the horizon line, to embrace the land, its soil, and its shapes. On a prominent site on Fifth Avenue, the Guggenheim's bold curves are a piece of Nature, of Truth

Left, top and bottom: Wyoming Valley Grammar School, Wyoming Valley, Wisconsin, 1956. Though the Wyoming School is in a rural area near Spring Green, Wright intended similar buildings to be built in the suburban Broadacre City.
Opposite: Herman T. Fasbender Medical Clinic, Hastings, Minnesota, 1957. The broad sheltering roof and the dominant chimney of this clinic echo the designs of Wright's suburban residential designs.

shouted in the face of dissimulation, hypocrisy, and venality. One can argue about its success for displaying certain kinds of art (as many artists did at the time in their own public denunciation of Wright's artwork for art), but it is as clear and brilliant a statement of architectural ideas as can be found anywhere.

In contrast, the V. C. Morris Gift Shop is less rhetorical, but just as critical of its surroundings. Modest on the exterior, it saves its proclamation of free space for the interior. It is hidden away on a small side street off Union Square in San Francisco, one of Wright's favorite regions and home of many of his friends and students; it was the only place outside Spring Green and Scottsdale where he established a field office in the 1950s. The shop's face to the city is subdued, reaching back to his early years with Adler and Sullivan in its direct simplicity: a plain tan brick wall fills the lot from side to side, and rises three stories. A single great arch outlined in four courses of brick penetrates the face; it is reminiscent of Sullivan's Stock Exchange building, of the entry and the fireplace of Wright's Heurtley House. It is a fragment of the muscular Richardsonian Romanesque arches that inspired Sullivan seventy years before.

From this statement of connection to his past and his mentors, Wright goes on to update the reference. The entry framed by this arch is set asymmetrically on the plain wall, accented by two ornamental filigrees of brick including lighting—one vertical, one horizontal. The entry itself is an abbreviated vault, reminiscent of the playroom he designed in his own Oak Park home for his children, but it is half glass and telescopes inward. Once inside, the simple curve of the exterior arch is transformed into a spiral ramp rising sinuously along the curving wall. The space is dramatically unexpected; from this forcibly narrowed entry sequence, the space lifts upward to a luminous ceiling of plastic hemispheres.

The design is, for Wright, an inspired compromise—a proof that he did not always

believe his own publicity about being an entirely original designer. When the context in which he was building was not the natural or suburban setting he preferred, then he proved he could be just as creative in adapting to a man-made urban context.

THE CITY EXALTED

If the Guggenheim Museum is Wright's inspired statement provoked by the folly of the centralized city, the Marin County Civic Center comes as close as any of his large buildings to proclaiming his ideal urbanism. It is, in fact, the capitol building of the Broadacre nation.

Marin County Civic Center could be seen as Wright's transmogrification of the U. S. Capitol in Washington, D.C., one of Democracy's great architectural symbols. In Wright's version, the two low wings focus on a central dome: the two wings represent the Administrative and Judicial functions, while the central dome represents Learning, in the form of a public library. But he makes a number of telling improvements based on his progressive philosophy. Instead of using Roman-Renaissance domes and palaces and their rigid symmetry as reference points, he uses the continuous arcades of Roman aqueducts as his primary motif. Instead of placing the building on a podium separating it from the earth, he blends its two wings into three hills rising from the bayside wetlands, responding appropriately to the natural topography. Nature is but a few easy steps from the building onto the hillside. The wings angle to meet nature, and the dome becomes a mechanical hinge, a fulcrum, between the two.

Finally, and most emphatically, he places this new type of civic symbol not at the focal point of the mono-centric city, but next to the highway, the major artery from San Francisco into Northern California and the northwest. This major civic monument is meant to be seen by the democratized car-mobile citizenry as a major presence along the vital highway network of the twentieth-century multi-centered suburban metropolis—idealized in Broadacre City. This is why his design fits into his grand plan for Broadacre City. As a civic center, he planned a golf course, racetracks, zoo, aquarium, planetarium, gardens, art museum, libraries, fairgrounds, and opera house as part of the civic center complex, all in line with his far ranging acceptance of the suburbs as a legitimate city form.

As with the Lindholm Service Station, the Price Tower, the Guggenheim Museum, and dozens of other buildings, Wright rethinks and reshapes the conventional administrative office building for the Marin County center. To bring light and air to every office, he slices a large atrium light well down the longitudinal section; this multi-story atrium doubles as the main interior circulation system. He also weaves the car through the building, creating large ground-floor arches for cars to pass from one side of the site to the other to park.

Wright produced several other large public designs which, if built, would have strengthened the argument for his approach to monumental architecture for the new city: Monona Terrace, a civic center on the lake in Madison, Wisconsin; the Arizona State Capitol in Phoenix; a university and opera house for Baghdad, the latter of which served as a model for Grady Gammage Memorial Auditorium in Tempe, Arizona.

WRIGHT AND THE TWENTY-FIRST CENTURY

Wright's always-provocative forms and ideas should form a basis of discussion for today. For all Wright's mythic and mystic rationale about nomads versus cave dwellers, the distinctions of centralization versus decentralization are useful. His embrace of the automobile and the suburbs is currently out of fashion; it was, however, progressive in its day, given the deteriorated nature of most city centers of the time. The cycles of opinion may yet change again.

But Wright also articulated a populist concern for nature—for ecology—that was to emerge and grow as popular movements after his death in 1959. His city of farmsteads that preserved nature was intended to avoid the irony of having "fish...for sale in this marketplace [when] there are none in its streams."[26] The widespread ecological movement born in the 1960s called for ways to allow people to live closer to true nature—setting aside land preserves and returning polluted rivers to a natural state. In the early twenty-first century the concept of producing food close to home is spreading (thereby saving the ecological costs of transporting food from halfway around the globe), as is growing fresher, less processed, and supposedly healthier food for sale in local markets. Wright's concept of a city of citizen-farmers living on their own acreage would require a drastic reshuffling of the city, but this growing concern today shows that his concept has been vindicated.

As a Wisconsin farm boy, Wright was more interested in nature expressed in practical agriculture, rather than in the recreational usages that evolved in the second half of the twentieth century. Nonetheless, the philosophical and spiritual justification for living in balance with nature, whether on one's own farm or during a backpacking trip through the Rocky Mountains, is the same. Just as he had understood the modern mass populace's desire for less formal living spaces in 1903, and their desire for open

kitchen-dining rooms in the 1936 Usonian house concept, Wright's intuitive formulation of a city that kept its citizens in touch with nature grasped a fundamental, post-industrial trend in human progress.

Likewise Wright's inclusion in Broadacre City of railroads speeding at 150 mph between cities pre-figured the need for a better, more efficient transportation system today. His concept of artisans' shops spread throughout the city foreshadowed the home offices spawned by the computer revolution of the 1990s. His batting average as a prophet was not perfect; he proposed nuclear-powered barges for mass transportation on rivers and lakes. And Broadacre City did not provide for the exponential growth in population and density that cities experienced in the second half of the twentieth century, after Wright's death. But the Wrightian ideal of decentralization sounds better every day. We can look at his public architecture today in a new light. From museums to schools to churches to gas stations to civic centers, the urbanist concept reflected in each has lessons for our cities today. •

Opposite: Midway Barns (1938) and Dairy and Machine Sheds (1947), Taliesin North, Spring Green, Wisconsin 1911, 1914-25.
Wright's concept of nature was practical, informed by his hard work as a youth on his uncles' farms. He designed these farm buildings on his Wisconsin estate as carefully as his house and studio to reflect the natural setting.

Reshaping Urban Landscapes

By David G. De Long

Frank Lloyd Wright's 1895 design for the Wolf Lake Amusement Park *(Chicago, unbuilt; fig. 1)* shows him fully conversant with principles of Beaux-Arts planning, allowing him to achieve grand unity at a vast scale. A symmetrical composition of water courts and esplanades linked by bridges and piers that extend out into the lake, it focuses on a circular island at its very center.[1] Barely four years later, in his proposal of 1899 for the Cheltenham Beach Resort *(Chicago, unbuilt; fig. 2)*, he combined elements similar in scale and complexity to Wolf Lake, but now arranged asymmetrically around less formal axes.[2] With Cheltenham, he initiated a series of designs for urban-scaled projects located within cities or in adjoining areas that offered visions of

an ever-grander unity, but without dependence on the formal axes of the Beaux-Arts. Had they been realized, these new systems of monumental order would have dramatically reshaped urban landscapes.[3]

Wright's early incorporation of Beaux-Arts principles has been much noted.[4] Ever observant, he would have learned them from his mentor, Louis H. Sullivan (1856–1924), who had studied at the Paris school, and he would have seen these principles demonstrated firsthand in the 1893 World's Columbian Exposition in Chicago. He continued for a time to apply these principles in designing inward-focused buildings within urban settings, as two of his most famous achievements (both demolished) attest:

the Larkin Company Administration Building (Buffalo, New York, 1902–06) and Midway Gardens (Chicago, 1913–14). In both, major elements remain individually legible, but are made subordinate to the axial, symmetrical organization that binds them together in a unified composition. Nor did Wright deny Beaux-Arts elements in his early work, instead suggesting that he was working his own variations.[5] During this same period, in undeveloped settings unconstrained by any urban context, he effected looser compositions of unified components, as in his proposal for the Lake Geneva Inn (Lake Geneva, Wisconsin, 1911; unbuilt). But none of these commissions provided opportunities for combining buildings of

multiple uses, so he began to design them on his own.

In 1922, following his return to the United States after prolonged stays in Japan, Wright briefly sought to re-establish his practice in Los Angeles. With its meteoric expansion then underway, the city must have seemed an ideal location for new work. Wright was appalled by what he regarded as the fragmented, insensitive development of its suburbs—what today would be called urban sprawl—and in 1923 he offered a corrective in what he called the Doheny Ranch development *(fig. 3)*.[6] With his design, he hoped to interest the wealthy owner of the ranch— Edward Laurence Doheny (1856–1935)—in developing the 411-acre tract in what is now

Opposite Fig. 1: Wolf Lake Amusement Park, Chicago, 1895 (unbuilt), aerial perspective (FLWF 9510.001).
Below Fig. 2: Cheltenham Beach Resort, Chicago, 1899 (unbuilt), aerial perspective (FLWF 9903.015).
Following pages, pp. 44–45, Fig. 3: Doheny Ranch development, Beverly Hills, California, 1923 (unbuilt), perspective (FLWF 2104.005).
Pp. 46–47, Fig. 4: San Marcos in the Desert, Chandler, Arizona, 1928 (unbuilt), aerial perspective (FLWF 2704.048).
Drawings of Frank Lloyd Wright are Copyright © 2008 The Frank Lloyd Wright Foundation, Taliesin West, Scottsdale, AZ.

Beverly Hills. What Wright envisioned was nothing less than an urbanized image of the suburb as one unified composition, with houses linked by structured roadways that were themselves architectural. Drawings for three prototypical houses that would be part of the development (labeled simply "A," "B," and "C") show in greater detail how these roadways were to be unifying extensions of the buildings, all clustered so as to stabilize the steep slopes while leaving much of the land untouched. Both the houses and roadways were to be constructed of custom-made concrete blocks, his newly proposed technique of prefabrication that he believed would reduce costs while enriching form through embossed patterns. Nothing came of Wright's proposal for the Doheny Ranch, yet later studies have shown that his perspectives adhered closely to the contours of the site, enhancing, but not obscuring, its salient features.

The Doheny Ranch development signaled important changes in Wright's work. It was larger in scale than any of his previous designs, and it seems to have been the first proposal by any major architect to integrate automobile roadways as a major part of the composition. The Doheny Ranch development also initiated a series of

experiments with new materials and new building techniques, some of which, in actual application, would prove more successful than others. And with his design for House "C," Wright began to explore new geometries, for he angled its walls in ways that infused it with new spatial energy. Earlier designs had incorporated angles, but as smaller attachments, such as bay windows or adjoining pavilions; now they were the defining component of the house itself.

While Wright came to champion the automobile for the freedom of movement it provided and continued to plan for the dispersed development it would facilitate, he was not naïve about its ultimate consequences. Realizing that people would choose to move to the suburbs whatever the long-term result, he later wrote, "America needs no help to Broadacre City. It will haphazard build itself. Why not plan it?"[7] And in 1954 he urged Americans to buy smaller cars that were less wasteful of fuel.[8]

Later in the 1920s, a real commission for a luxurious resort south of Phoenix provided an opportunity for Wright to expand upon aspects of his Doheny project: San Marcos in the Desert (Chandler, Arizona, 1928; unbuilt). The onset of the Great Depression in 1929 doomed the project just as construction was about to begin,

and suburban development stretching out from Phoenix now obscures the site.[9]

For San Marcos, Wright planned an urban-scaled complex of interconnected units that reinforced the contours of the sloping site (fig. 4). Stretching for more than 1,000 feet along the base of nearby mountains, rows of individual suites, each with its own terrace, stepped back along the hill. They angled out from a central core containing lounge and restaurant facilities, and at that central location the orthogonal lines of the suites intersected in such a way as to generate triangular shapes of extraordinary richness. Connections to detached dwellings at each end further expanded the composition, and additional buildings (seen behind in the perspective) suggested still greater scale. The resort was to have been built of Wright's prefabricated concrete blocks, here fluted to capture and reflect what Wright regarded as the dotted line of the desert, thus animating the structure as a whole and further uniting it with its setting. Given the nature of the project, roadways played a secondary role, but Wright still included them as part of his design, as seen in other drawings for the project.

With his design for San Marcos, Wright achieved monumental unity without recourse to formal Beaux-Arts methods, fulfilling a potential only barely suggested by the Cheltenham project. It constituted a new approach to planning with untapped potential for urban applications. In later designs employing triangular geometries, Wright spoke of the more generous angles generated by its shapes—120 degrees instead of the more conventional 90—as having "more fertility and flexibility where human movement is concerned than the square."[10] It was the same at larger scale, where informally angled axes facilitated freer movement, in contrast to the more restrictive paths generated by typical Beaux-Arts axes.

Opportunities for large-scale planning incorporating the automobile remained elusive, so again Wright assigned one to himself, but

now with the encouragement of local colleagues.[11] The resulting proposal for Monona Terrace (Madison, Wisconsin, 1938; unbuilt) appears at first to revert to Beaux-Arts principles with its more formal axes and balanced symmetry (fig. 5). Partly this was in response to the regular but unbound plan of Madison, which Wright wanted to resolve with his urban-scaled terminal. But he reversed normal Beaux-Arts practice by locating civic elements below rather than above his broad terrace, and its semi-circular shape was generated by multiple levels of roadways and parking underneath. Within this enclosure were to be auditoria for concerts and theater as well as law courts and related facilities, and at the base of the structure a marina was to tie directly to Lake Monona, further unifying the city with its agreeable setting.[12] The terrace itself was to be enriched with overlooks to other landscaped terraces below, sources of light and air for the facilities contained within. Although this first proposal was not built, it captured the attention of Madison's citizens; Wright continued to revise it in the years that followed, and in 1997, almost forty years after his death, a modified version—smaller and less complex—was at last realized.

Wright's manipulation of circular geometries to accommodate the automobile can be traced back to his proposal for the Gordon Strong Automobile Objective (Sugarloaf, Maryland, 1924–25; unbuilt).[13] Its program called for extensive indoor parking, and in an article on parking garages that Wright was sent to facilitate his planning, circular spirals were touted as an ideal form, although at that time none had actually been built. Wright's solution for the Automobile Objective went far beyond a mere parking garage, however, for he manipulated the spiral to provide overlooks to the surrounding countryside and give dramatic shape to its mountain setting while also enclosing a planetarium inside. The idea of the spiral remained fixed in his mind, especially in urban-scaled applications involving the

automobile and its necessary roadways, as later proposals show.

With his 1940 design for Crystal Heights in Washington, D.C. (unbuilt), Wright reconfigured the angled geometries of his project for San Marcos in the Desert for a truly urban setting (fig. 6). As with Monona Terrace, Wright generated its shapes partly in response to adjoining street patterns, but here those patterns were the angled diagonals of Washington's plan. Yet his scheme was radically different from the conservative buildings that characterized Washington at that time, and its connected

Within the image:
OLIN TERRACE · MONONA AVENUE · MONONA AVE. · FOR PARKING. · RACE · ROAD DEPOT · COST $17,500,000, RAISED BY —? (SEE KAUFMANN À LA PITTSBURG.) · "THE CITY GOES TO THE LAKE" · SEVEN MONTHS WATERDOMES, FIVE MONTHS EVERGREENS, INSTEAD. · WILLSON ST. · CARROLL · RAMP

buildings evoked a dynamic, rather than a static, monumentality. It was more fluid in form and more in alignment with the positive energy of a twentieth-century city as Wright interpreted it.

Within the triangle defined by bordering streets, Wright proposed a multi-level parking structure to support a monumental terrace.[14] Shops along the base of the terraced structure, brought into focus by a cinema at its point, would have provided an active, pedestrian-friendly facade. The interlocking towers enclosing the far side of the terrace were to contain hotels and apartments, their angled shapes developed in plan by rotating superimposed squares around central supports, much like his earlier proposal of individual towers for St. Mark's in the Bouwerie (New York City, 1929; unbuilt), but here the towers were to be interwoven with stunning effect. Wright described the faceted walls of glass that would result as having a crystalline appearance—thus his name for the project.

In addition to banquet halls, restaurants, and other facilities serving the hotel, the complex was also to contain bowling alleys and an art gallery, with tunnels below providing generous access for services. The visionary aspect of the scheme must have concerned the project's backers, and its radical modernity would have alarmed the guardians of Washington's conservative image whatever its complications, but the official reason given for cancellation of

Above Fig. 5: Monona Terrace civic center, Madison, Wisconsin, 1938 (first scheme, unbuilt), aerial perspective (FLWF 3909.002).

Drawing of Frank Lloyd Wright is Copyright © 2008 The Frank Lloyd Wright Foundation, Taliesin West, Scottsdale, AZ.

CRYSTAL HEIGHTS WASHINGTON D.C. FRANK LLOYD WRIGHT ARCHITEC

the project was its height, which exceeded the city's mandated limit.

In 1947, Wright proposed an urban project far larger and more complicated than even his design for Crystal Heights: Pittsburgh Point Park (Pittsburgh, Pennsylvania; unbuilt). That year, with the backing of Edgar Kaufmann (who had commissioned Fallingwater), civic leaders invited Wright to envision how an industrial area near the city's downtown core might be redeveloped. In response, Wright conceived a new core as one gigantic megastructure that would have

Above Fig. 6: Crystal Heights, Washington, D.C., 1940 (unbuilt), aerial perspective (FLWF 4016.001).
Left Fig. 7: Pittsburgh Point Park civic center, Pittsburgh, Pennsylvania, 1947 (first scheme, unbuilt), aerial perspective (FLWF 4821.004).
Drawings of Frank Lloyd Wright are Copyright © 2008 The Frank Lloyd Wright Foundation. Taliesin West, Scottsdale, AZ.

dwarfed the buildings of the city's adjacent downtown *(fig. 7)*.[15] Wright shaped his scheme in response to the triangular site at the junction of the Allegheny and Monongahela rivers, with esplanades along the two banks bordered with shops, restaurants, and even a zoo. At the point of the site he proposed a circular terrace to house aquaria, swimming pools, a marina, and a grand restaurant. He wanted to replace existing bridges over the rivers with new, more dramatic spans that would become an integral part of the design, each double-decked, with commercial traffic below to be separated from automobile and pedestrian traffic above. Where they met at the center of the site, he outlined a vast multi-level traffic interchange that would link with Pittsburgh's existing streets. Above the interchange, a spiral parking structure was to rise twelve levels; two smaller spirals behind would provide express access up and down. A mid-rise building for city and county offices

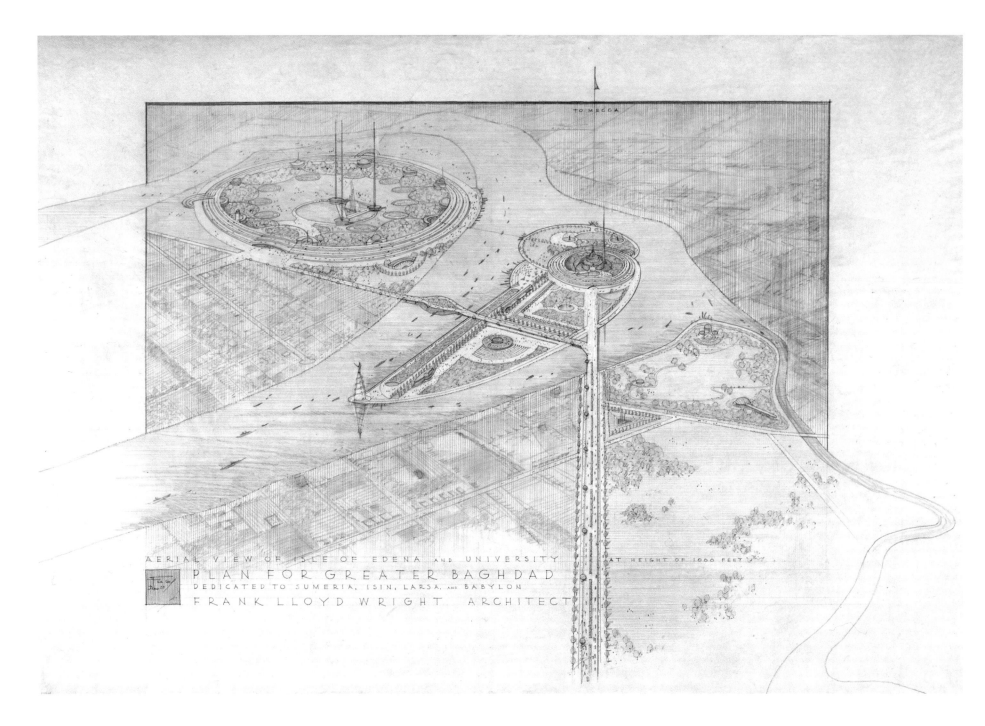

AERIAL VIEW OF ISLE OF EDENA AND UNIVERSITY AT HEIGHT OF 1000 FEET

PLAN FOR GREATER BAGHDAD
DEDICATED TO SUMERIA, ISIN, LARSA, AND BABYLON

FRANK LLOYD WRIGHT ARCHITECT

Fig. 8: Plan for Greater Baghdad, Iraq, 1957 (unbuilt),
aerial perspective (FLWF 5733.008).

Drawing of Frank Lloyd Wright is Copyright © 2008 The Frank Lloyd Wright
Foundation, Taliesin West, Scottsdale, AZ.

projected out from the front of the parking spiral, with an illuminated 500-foot-tall spire rising above.

Elaborate drawings that Wright prepared reveal staggering details. The multiple lanes of the wide parking ramp were to be edged with a landscape band that he hoped would ameliorate noise and exhaust, and three multi-acre levels of parking below the spiral would have accommodated even more cars. Major components were to be contained within the central volume of the spiral, including a winter garden and aquarium at the top with a sports arena, a concert hall, a planetarium, an opera house, a convention hall, and a cinema on descending levels below.

In part the scheme is symmetrical, but multiple levels of roadways and asymmetrically angled terraces energize that symmetry, and the civic facilities contained within the spiral were more freely disposed. So, too, were vehicular approach ramps to each of the internal components, as were inclined elevators at the perimeter that would have provided pedestrian access. The project's size and complexity must have seemed totally unrealistic to its sponsors, and it failed to gain needed support. Yet in the years that followed, gigantic highway interchanges built in urban areas have demonstrated that structures of comparable scale were possible—what Wright did was show how they could be put to better civic purpose. A simpler scheme that he submitted later also remained undeveloped.

In 1957, fewer than two years before he died just short of his 92nd birthday, Wright proposed a still grander, but more realistic, scheme: the Plan for Greater Baghdad. Commissioned by the government to plan a new opera house for the city, he quickly expanded the program to include a broad range of cultural facilities as well as a new university, again assigning himself an urban-scaled problem of the sort he clearly relished. Mammoth parking spirals again figured in the scheme *(fig. 8)*, but now held to three levels,

with each less complicated than what he had proposed for Pittsburgh; on drawings for Baghdad, Wright termed them "parking ziggurats," one of several acknowledgments of a local culture he had long admired.

Wright chose to locate the opera house itself on an island in the Tigris River, placing it at the upper tip and surrounding it with one of the ziggurats that, he explained, would provide both shade for the parked cars and embanked protection against floods. An elaborate garden within the spiral was planned as a setting for the opera house, to which Wright added a second auditorium and a planetarium. Circular extensions projecting out over the river—to contain additional gardens and a marina—gave clear shape to the upper part of the complex. Additional elements shown extending down along the spine of the island—to include a sculpture museum, an art gallery, and a "grand bazaar"—further enlarged the scale of Wright's unified scheme.

Wright planned new avenues to connect the opera and related facilities with a second ziggurat in the distance. There the three-level parking spiral was to enclose the new university and be linked to twelve structures contained within: a library, two athletic centers, and separate groupings for nine faculties. At the center, three 500-foot tall television towers rising from a circular pool would have provided a vertical accent.

With his design for Baghdad, Wright again gave powerful shape to an urban landscape, manipulating buildings and roadways to achieve monumental unity. As new cities being built in the Middle East now show, Wright's scheme was realistic in scope, but bolder and more coherent in form than most of those now planned. However, the overthrow of Iraq's government in 1958 led to the abandonment of Wright's project.[16]

Wright's urban-scaled projects, beginning in 1895 and extending over a period of more than 60 years, define a remarkable trajectory. All are

strongly ordered, all relate to and even clarify forms inherent in their settings, all depend on basic Euclidian shapes, as do his other designs: compositions generated by squares, circles, and triangles. Yet as a comparison of Wolf Lake and Baghdad show, those shapes, while similar in derivation, came to be differently organized, leaving the predictable symmetries of the Ecole des Beaux-Arts far behind. Even his master plan for Florida Southern College (Lakeland, Florida, 1938, partly built), where he experimented with a looser organization of parts, was generated from those basic shapes. He disparaged freer geometries, as his damning criticism of a design Bruce Goff (1904–1982)—otherwise a respected colleague—reveals.[17] He would probably have regarded current work by Frank Gehry, Daniel Libeskind, and other neo-expressionists as ridiculously undisciplined. After all, Wright's designs epitomized another era. Yet his visionary proposals offer classic paradigms for an all-too-elusive urban order, and as such they remain unsurpassed. •

Notes: My research on Frank Lloyd Wright over the past quarter-century would not have been possible without the extraordinary support I have received from the Frank Lloyd Wright Foundation and from the Archives at Taliesin West in Scottsdale, Arizona. I am particularly grateful to Bruce Brooks Pfeiffer, Director of the Frank Lloyd Wright Archives, and to his colleagues, Margo Stipe and Oskar Munoz. I also wish to thank all those at Taliesin West who have made my stays so very enjoyable, in particular, Indira Berndtson.

Frank Lloyd Wright: Selected Plans

By Kathryn Smith

Frank Lloyd Wright's public buildings, the majority of which were erected after 1938, present an astounding range of forms, materials, and structural systems—from the Price Tower with its faceted facades of glass and copper, to the austere abstraction of Unity Temple with its exposed concrete surface; from the Annunciation Greek Orthodox Church with its efflorescence of Byzantine ornamentation, to the Guggenheim Museum with its spiraling ramp culminating in a top-lit glass dome. Is it conceivable that this unlimited variety of design ideas came from the imagination of only one architect? At first glance, it appears impossible to discern a consistent set of principles or a progressive design evolution within this body of work until proceeding to an analysis of the plans. Astonishingly, all of these structures were generated from a single geometric form and manipulated by a few fundamental strategies to create an almost endless number of buildings.

It was not by accident that Wright chose the square as his insignia, for from this shape he generated his architectural vocabulary. For the octagon and hexagon, he simply sliced off the corners of the square; the triangle was formed by bisecting the square on the diagonal; and the circle is formed by rotating the square around its center point—the act of rotation creating the circumference of a circle. Equally remarkable, there are three distinct periods where particular geometries predominate: orthogonal planning between 1887 and 1922, diagonal planning from 1923 until 1937; and circular planning from 1938 to 1959. During the last twenty years of his career, Wright became a virtuoso by mastering all three, using each interchangeably, and in his most masterful designs, such as the Guggenheim Museum, employing all three simultaneously.

A major strategy used from the very beginning was rotation around a vertical axis, either a solid core or a hollow one. Rotating a square balcony 45 degrees within a square, for instance, created the original assembly hall of the Hillside Home School. The Price Tower, based on the 1929 project for St. Mark's in the Bouwerie, applies the same principle, yet in this instance, the rotation is 30 degrees around a solid—the structural/service trunk.

After 1932, as Wright explored ever more complex spatial relationships, especially in response to landscape features, he moved from rotation around a center point to pivoting from a point on the outer edge; the obvious result was also a shift from symmetry to asymmetry. At the Unitarian Meeting House, the residential wing is pivoted 45 degrees from a point on the edge of the main body of the building to enclose the garden. When applied to programs of even greater complexity such as the campus of Florida Southern College, the strategy is difficult to discern at first. The master plan was laid out on an orthogonal grid, then Wright shifted one section 30 degrees off a point on the upper edge to the southwest, and a second section yet again 30 degrees off the first diagonal axis in the same direction. The result— what the architect called "occult symmetry"—

is a sweeping arc in the direction of the sun and toward the main landscape feature—Lake Hollingsworth.

During the Oak Park years, Wright applied a rationalist methodology to design by analyzing function and creating typologies. One of these— the bi-nuclear plan for public buildings—sustained him throughout his career. By establishing a hierarchy from the primary function to supporting spaces, or what Louis I. Kahn later referred to as the "servant and the served," Wright was free to design a distinct form for each, usually joined together by a circulation spine. This idea evolved from the Oak Park Studio with its octagonal drafting room and library joined by the reception room, to the Larkin Building with its rectangular office block linked to the employees' lounge, to the Johnson Wax Building with its top-lit great workroom connected to the garage/ service wing, to the Guggenheim Museum, with the main gallery rotunda separated from the smaller monitor by the entrance loggia.

After his move to Taliesin in 1911, Wright's planning became less inventive and more formal, even containing suggestions of Classicism. This direction is best illustrated in his orthogonal compositions for Midway Gardens and the Imperial Hotel designed as they were according to the strict symmetry of axial organization. Yet his relocation to California in 1923 after his long sojourn in Japan marked the critical turning point in Wright's planning development. In a series of 1920s projects that were never built, such as the Tahoe Summer Colony, San Marcos in the Desert, the Steel Cathedral for One Million People, and St. Mark's in the Bouwerie, Wright engaged in radical experiments with diagonal planning to create new dynamic spatial experiences, laying the groundwork for an explosion of commissions in the 1940s and 1950s.

Although some well-known examples of the late work, for example, Kalita Humphreys Theater and Beth Sholom Synagogue, derive from the experimentation of the 1920s, the last two decades of Wright's career are notable for

his use of circular planning. It is as if the fundamental strategies of rotation and pivoting finally culminate in their logical conclusion—the circle. Remarkably, very late buildings such as the V. C. Morris Gift Shop and Grady Gammage Memorial Auditorium recall earlier Oak Park plans as they are also generated from rotation around a vertical axis. While some critics view the full sweep of Wright's seventy-year career as eccentric and unclassifiable, indeed, from the perspective of planning, he never wavered from a set of unifying principles that shaped his design process. •

Selected Plans:

1. Midway Gardens
2. Unitarian Meeting House
3. Larkin Company Administration Building
4. S. C. Johnson & Son Administration Building (Johnson Wax Building)
5. Unity Temple
6. Solomon R. Guggenheim Museum
7. Taliesin West
8. Florida Southern College
9. Price Tower
10. Beth Sholom Synagogue
11. Ann Pfeiffer Chapel
12. Annunciation Greek Orthodox Church

Pages 56–61: Drawings of Frank Lloyd Wright are Copyright © 2008 The Frank Lloyd Wright Foundation, Taliesin West, Scottsdale, AZ. Archival photographs are Courtesy The Frank Lloyd Wright Foundation, Taliesin West, Scottsdale, AZ.

Frank Lloyd Wright Home and Studio, Oak Park, Illinois, 1889-97.
Left: Wright built his office in 1897 on busy Chicago Avenue next to his suburban home, visible behind the office entry. The taller octagon (left) lighted the drafting room, and the smaller octagon (right) contained his office library.
Opposite left: Office waiting room, looking into drafting room;
Middle: Drafting room;
Right: Interior of library.

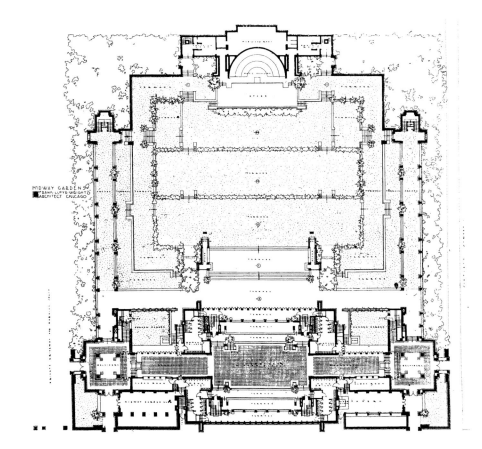

Midway Gardens (1914)

The bi-laterally symmetrical plan shows evidence of Classicism with the main axis terminating in the music pavilion, the most important area of Midway Gardens, where orchestral music and dance performances were the main entertainment for the diners. The major secondary cross-axis separates the outdoor summer garden from the minor enclosed winter garden, while an additional secondary cross-axis cuts a circulation spine through the center of the indoor restaurant. At Midway Gardens, Wright paid homage to his geometric vocabulary—the cube, the pyramid, and the sphere—in freestanding sculptures of sprites, each holding aloft a three-dimensional figure.

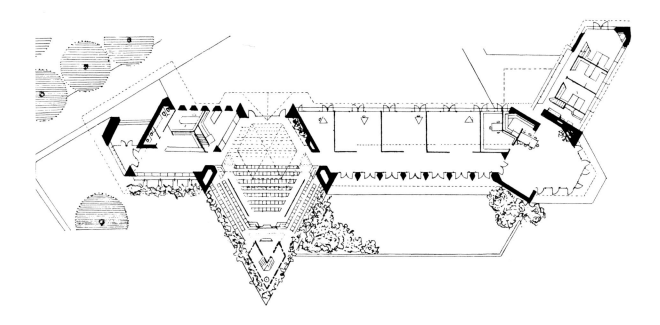

Unitarian Meeting House (1947)

The program called for a meeting room for worship and social activities, classrooms, and a residence for the minister. The meeting room consists of a parallelogram composed of 30/60-degree angles superimposed over a circulation spine that contains the educational spaces. The residential wing—not built as designed—is pivoted at a point along the outer edge at a 30-degree angle. Wright's diagonal planning provides flexibility to the multi-functional spaces.

Larkin Company Administration Building (1903)

The bi-nuclear plan applied to a large modern mail-order company. The main office block is defined as a rectangle with articulated corner stair towers and a mezzanine-ringed atrium rising the full height of the building. The main entrance bisects the two zones: executives and employees working in the office tower with rooms for library, locker area, and toilets in the subordinate mass. The circulation spine allows entrance from either the front or rear with a semi-circular reception desk at the central location.

S. C. Johnson & Son Administration Building (1936)

Almost exactly thirty years after the Larkin Building, Wright conceived of what he called the feminine version of the bi-nuclear plan for a major manufacturer of household products. The company hierarchy of executives, managers, and clerical staff is located within an enormous top-lit great workroom. In this instance, the automobile becomes an important element with an entrance driveway separating the workroom from the secondary unit (the garage with exercise deck and squash court above). While the plan uses a square module, curvilinear features are introduced, primarily with the columns supporting the translucent ceiling.

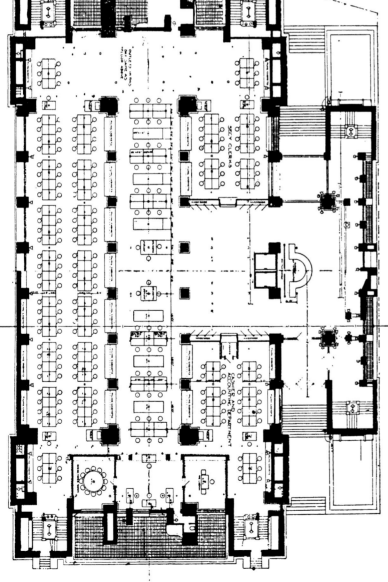

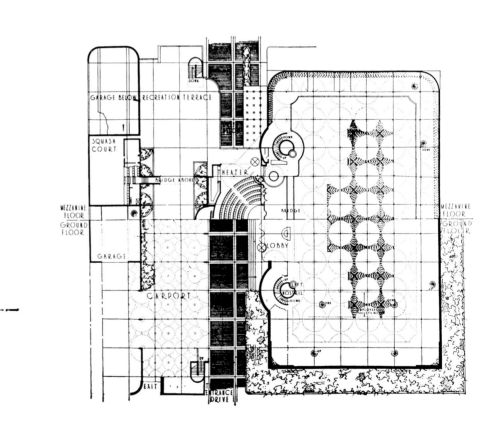

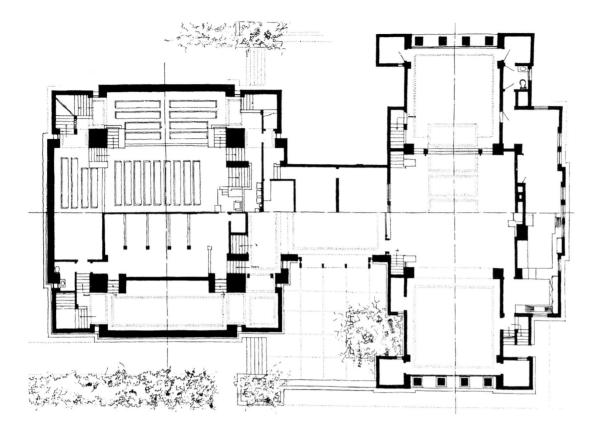

Unity Temple (1906)
The most totally resolved of the bi-nuclear plans consists of a perfect cube joined to a rectangular volume. The plan reflects the diverse nature of the program: a sacred space for the congregation to worship, an area for socializing and educational programs, and an entrance from two sides protected from the noise and bustle of the surrounding streets. The plan is bi-laterally symmetrical and organized along a main longitudinal axis. The sacred room is a symphony of the square as every detail down to the smallest elements is worked out according to this theme.

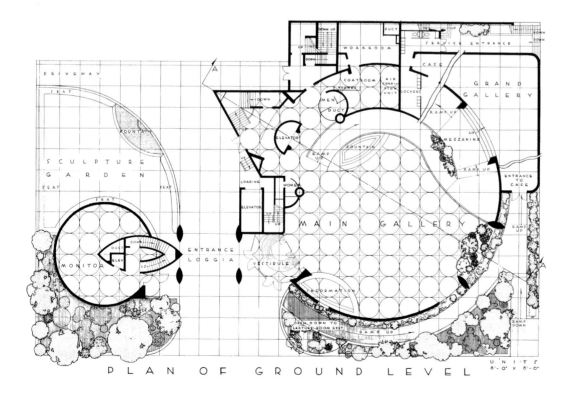

PLAN OF GROUND LEVEL

UNITS
8'-0" x 8'-0"

Solomon R. Guggenheim Museum (1956)
The most complex of the bi-nuclear plans reflects Wright's virtuosity with geometry by 1943, when design development was initiated. While the basic elements of a major and minor mass are present, the subtleties are multiple. The main gallery consists of a circle inscribed within a square with the addition of a triangular projection. While the main movement is a spiraling circulation spine, diagonal planning is reflected in the entrance, 30/60 degrees off the street grid along Fifth Avenue. The major axis is diagonal, crossing from the elevator core through the rotunda and out a window to the street beyond. Wright planned an interior driveway separating the two units, but this feature was lost in a subsequent alteration.

Taliesin West (1937)

At Taliesin West, to take advantage of sweeping views across Paradise Valley to the southwest, Wright rotated a square 90 degrees around its center point, bisected it on the diagonal, and superimposed an orthogonal organization of units —drafting room, dining room, main residence, apprentice rooms, and guest cottage—aligned with this longitudinal axis. The entrance drive, workshops, Wright's studio, the upper section of the apprentice court, and the projecting garden prow all conform to the geometry of the rotated square. The two geometries—orthogonal and diagonal—work together; the first providing a clear order to each function, the second bringing the desert floor and the mountaintops beyond into the composition of the camp. The underlying rotated square became more evident when Wright enlarged the camp: first with a cabaret and then a music pavilion, placing them on the 45-degree axis balancing the triangular garden prow.

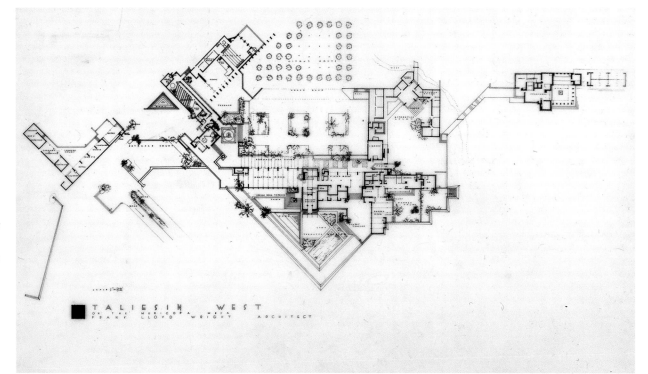

Florida Southern College (1937–54)

One of Wright's most sophisticated examples of diagonal planning on the scale of a master plan is for a small college on the shore of a Florida sinkhole lake. While addressing an academic program for the arts and sciences, Wright was first seized by the natural features of a citrus orchard (on an 36-foot orthogonal grid) and a circular lake. For symbolism, he derived his basic plan of a 18-foot square module from the orchard— mimicking in architecture the agrarian order. He placed the most important unit—the Ann Pfeiffer Chapel—in the exact center of the site. There are several longitudinal axes—one extending into the lake between the outdoor theater and swimming pool and the other directly through the center of the waterdome. Using the strategy of pivoting from the outer edge, he rotated the science-music unit 30 degrees to the southwest, and again rotated the library another 30 degrees off the first diagonal axis in the same direction. The pivoting follows the direction of the light, conveying symbolic meaning to the Florida composition, which Wright named "Child of the Sun." The master plan was only partially completed.

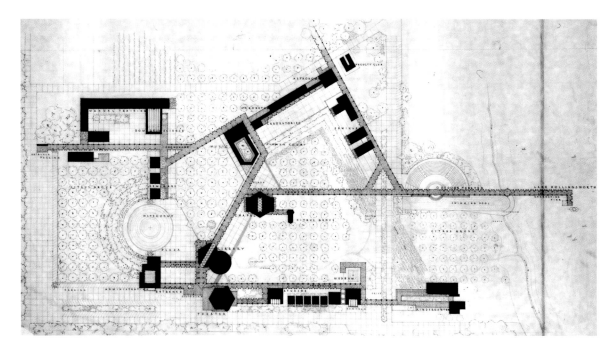

Price Tower (1952)

Wright adapted Price Tower from its model, St. Mark's in the Bouwerie, originally designed as an apartment house. The conversion to an office building with apartment units required some adjustments to the plan, but remained consistent with his original concept. The tower rotates around a structural core and primarily derives from a square rotated 30 degrees within a square, creating four quadrants, each presenting a different facade. This system allowed the architect to site the building in keeping with location, climate, and orientation to the sun. Using quadrants, planned on a diamond (parallelogram) module, eliminated hallways and made maximum use of space.

Beth Sholom Synagogue

(1954) Derived from an ambitious earlier project for a "Cathedral for One Million People," also known as the Steel Cathedral, the plan has been scaled down and adapted as a synagogue. The centralized plan is derived from an equilateral triangle circumscribed within a distended hexagon. Not obvious from the ground-floor plan is the fact that this is an inverted bi-nuclear plan, where the auxiliary rooms have been grouped together and placed in the basement. The result allows the main volume to be freely enclosed within a translucent skin, bringing the mystery of light into the service.

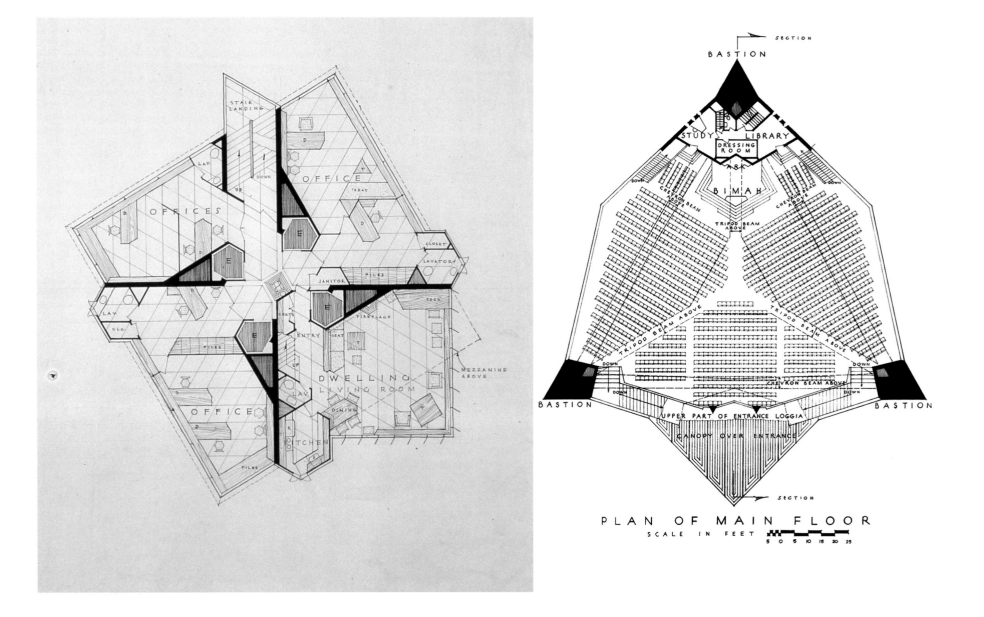

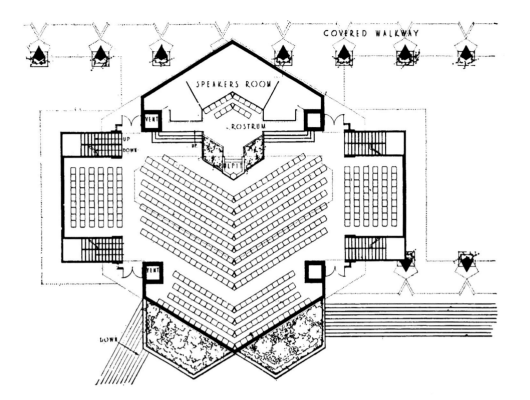

Ann Pfeiffer Chapel (1938)

This unit, which was to serve as both a chapel and an auditorium for a small private college, is two stories, with balconies and choir loft above. The plan is a modified cruciform consisting of an extended hexagon imposed over a rectangle. Although they appear dissimilar, Pfeiffer Chapel derives from Unity Temple in the cruciform orientation and the use of square pillars at the corners. In both, the columns are structural, but at Pfeiffer Chapel they also function as ventilation stacks.

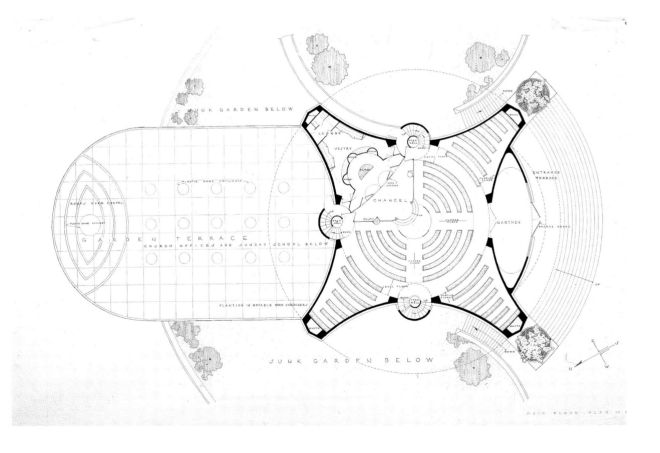

Annunciation Greek Orthodox Church (1956)

An ingenious version of a centralized cruciform plan, with a circle over a Greek cross composed of four circular segments. This is one of Wright's most pure geometric compositions and reflects his development from the Oak Park period to his late work where the simplicity of the circle is allowed to stand on its own.

The Buildings

Unity Temple

Oak Park, Illinois, 1904

In the center of his hometown of Oak Park, Illinois, Frank Lloyd Wright designed a revolutionary church structure. While it shared an aesthetic with his comfortable Prairie Style residences in the surrounding neighborhoods, it developed a distinctive public version of those Prairie ideas.

Right: The architecture expressed the slab-like forms of its innovative concrete structure.
Far right: Intentionally avoiding the motifs and symbols of traditional religion, Wright exploited natural light and abstract geometry to create the serene meeting room.

Above, left: Entry from the main street. Above, right: Wright designed all ornamental fixtures, including this light,
to harmonize with the architecture. Opposite: The building included the meeting room at left, and the community room at right.
Planters typically adorned walls and landscape features in Wright designs of this era.

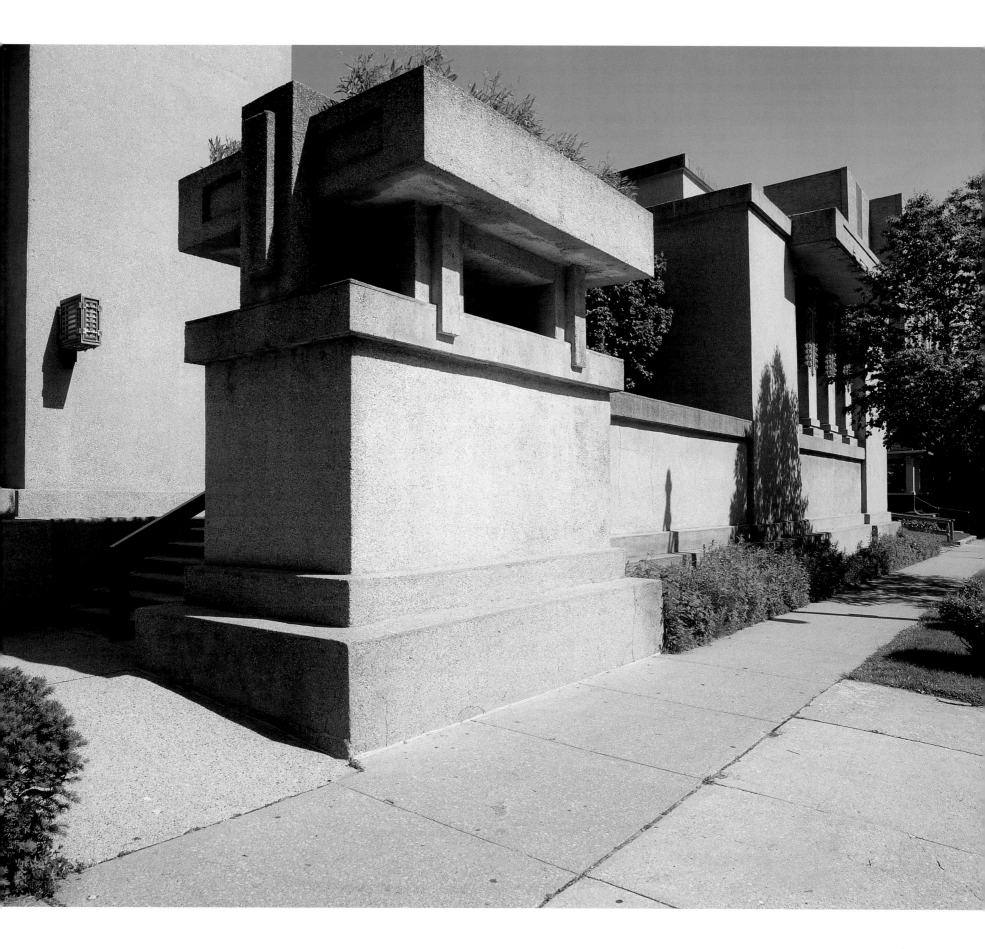

Above, left: Art glass light fixtures with globes contrasted the building's rectilinear geometry.

Above, right: Ceiling skylights and lighting fixtures.

Opposite: Congregants entered the meeting room by walking up the stairs flanking the platform.

Above, left: Balconies circle the central space. Above, right: View of skylights over meeting room.
Opposite: View from platform looking out to congregation.

Taliesin North

Spring Green, Wisconsin, 1911, 1914-25

Wright's estate was much more than a home; it encompassed an office, farm, school, guest houses, theaters, and dining rooms that supported an entire community of architects, artists, and craftspeople in the rural splendor of Spring Green, Wisconsin.

Right: The main house sits on the brow of a hill. Far right: Wright remodeled the estate constantly over his lifetime as his community grew and changed.

Living room of the main house. Above, left: The hearth was the focal point of gatherings, music performances, and Wright's meetings with his apprentices. Above, right: Windowed alcoves extend the sense of continuous space. Opposite: Built near the end of his Prairie Style years, Taliesin showed new directions for Wright's design in its bold asymmetrical volumes and dramatic blend of ceiling forms.

Taliesin, main house, living rooms. Above, clockwise from upper left: Polished stone floors echo the natural setting; living area also seen on opposite page; Wright uses both plain glass and patterned screens for exterior window walls; built-in furniture reinforces the flow of space. Opposite: By avoiding the use of conventional walls, Wright creates a flowing interior that blends easily with the natural scenery outside. Here he uses stone pillars, low partition walls, and glass to shape the space.

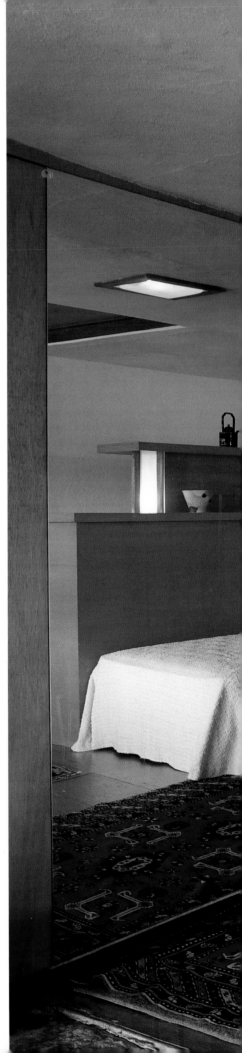

Taliesin includes suites of bedrooms for Wright, his family, guests, and apprentices.
The sophisticated integration of indoor and outdoor spaces, views, work areas, lounges, and
sleeping areas is seen in this suite.

Above and opposite: Bedroom suite. Art, stonework, plaster walls, views, and wood trim
combine with built-in furniture and varied ceiling heights to distinguish this space.

Left: The main house seen from the hilltop, with the porte-cochere at center. Above: The balcony off suite was extended from its original length to create an even more dramatic cantilever.

Left, top: The tower building on the hilltop above Taliesin's main house served originally as a stable for horses and cows, and as a garage. It was expanded over the years as the Fellowship grew and needed more quarters, dining rooms, and work areas.
Left, bottom and right: Living room. Opposite: Dining room.

Over the years, Wright remodeled and reused the buildings neighboring Taliesin that he had designed as the Hillside School for his aunts in 1902. Left: The original buildings display the wide eaves and broad windows of many of his Prairie houses. Above: The buildings nestled into the rolling hillside.

Above, left: Though built of rough ashlar stone, the crisp geometries of the architecture stand out.
Above, right: The three-story wing adapts to the natural topography. Bottom right: Bridge and roadway. Opposite: As a complex
of pavilions linked by bridges, the Hillside School established the forms seen at the 1907 Coonley House by Wright.

Assembly rooms throughout Taliesin underscore the communal nature of the complex.

Above: Three views show Wright's integration of spaces and levels to accommodate the Hillside building's sloping site.

Opposite: The stone hearth becomes the center of the space.

Previous pages: Hillside Home buildings. Above, left: Dining room. Above, right, and opposite: In the drafting room bold trusses demonstrate Wright's ability to turn a structural necessity into an extraordinary spatial composition. He incorporates skylights into the structure to bring even lighting to the tabletops of his draftsmen.

Wright arranges seating and terraces around the thrust stage of a small theater.
Though the structure is basically rectangular, Wright introduces oblique angles to create good site lines.

Theater. The rich pattern of lines in the wood ceiling structure is reflected decoratively in the curtain.

Wright designed the Riverview Terrace Restaurant in the vicinity of Taliesin North in 1953. It was completed after his death by
Taliesin Associated Architects. Top left: Entry. Bottom left: Facade overlooking river. Above, right: A solid masonry base contrasting with a light,
ornamented roof was a frequent Wrightian motif. Opposite: Dining room.

Previous pages: Romeo and Juliet Tower (1896). Wright believed that nature, in the form of agriculture, was essential to a healthy society.
His architectural community was also a farming community, and he designed stables, silos, windmills, and barns for Taliesin.
Above, opposite, and following pages: Midway Barns, the functional farm structures built from 1938 and 1947, responded to the site as effectively
as any of his residential designs. Circular stone building is a milk tower.

A. D. German Warehouse

Richland, Wisconsin, 1915

A warehouse presented Wright with a stimulating challenge. As a large structure, it had a monumental urban presence on the city street. As a utilitarian structure, it had few windows. It challenged Wright to draw on new sources to interpret these requirements. The concrete structure is expressed on the facade behind the brick, but so is the tapestry-like ornament on the top floor.

Left, top: As his interest in the Prairie Style waned, Wright looked for inspiration to the Pre-Columbian American
architecture of the Mayans for their monumental geometries and delicate ornament. Left, bottom: Side-street facade with delivery entry.
Right: Delivery entry. Opposite: Concrete columns with spread capitals create a public entry and facade.

S. C. Johnson & Son Administration Building

(Johnson Wax Building) Racine, Wisconsin, 1936

In Wright's ideal city, offices and factories were to have as much architectural distinction as museums and churches. Built as interest in Wright's career was reviving, the Johnson Wax headquarters offered a stunning view of the future.

Right: Entry porte-cochere between buildings. Opposite: Tall concrete columns supporting skylights create a luminous ceiling—an updated version of the 1903 Larkin Company offices.

Photograph this page is Courtesy The Frank Lloyd Wright Foundation, Taliesin West, Scottsdale, AZ. Photograph opposite is Copyright © 2008 Paul Rocheleau.

Above: Aerial view of Johnson Wax Building. The main office space is in the building at right. The thin horizontal strips between the brick walls are formed with glass tubes to let light into the building. Far left: A research tower was added in 1944. Its floors, visible here during construction, cantilevered like the branches of a tree off the central core. Left: The daring engineering of the slender columns and broad capitals of the main office space violated existing building codes, offering Wright a public opportunity to dramatically prove the strength of his concept. Building a sample column, he loaded it beyond the required code requirements. Wright stands at right, Herbert F. Johnson at left.

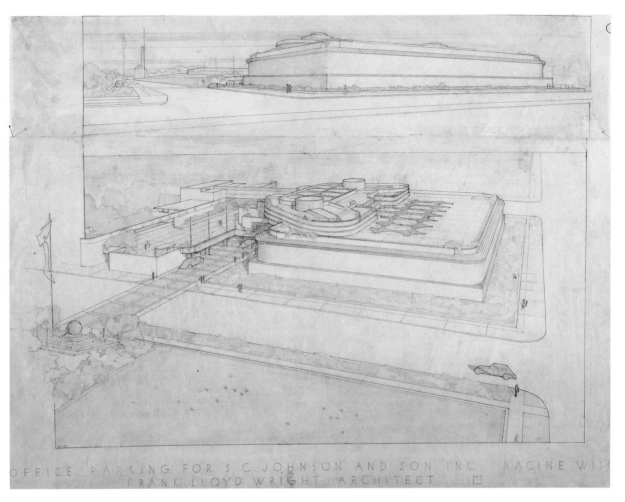

OFFICE PARKING FOR S C JOHNSON AND SON INC   RACINE WISC
FRANK LLOYD WRIGHT ARCHITECT   □

Above right, top:
Drawing of Johnson
Wax Building.
Right: Cut away
drawing of the main
office space.

Photographs (this page and opposite)
are Courtesy The Frank Lloyd Wright
Foundation, Taliesin West,
Scottsdale, AZ. Drawings of Frank
Lloyd Wright are Copyright © 2008
The Frank Lloyd Wright Foundation,
Taliesin West, Scottsdale, AZ.

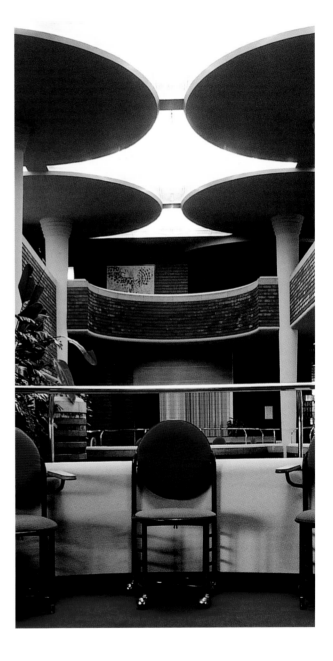

Left: Main office space. Wright also designed the
furniture for the building. Above: Side chair.

Photograph at left is Courtesy The Frank Lloyd Wright Foundation, Taliesin West, Scottsdale, AZ.

Photograph above is Copyright © 2008 Paul Rocheleau.

Above left: Glass tunnel of Pyrex tubing connects wings of building. Above right: Glass dome of office reception area.

Opposite: The building's curving forms are similar to the Streamline Moderne style popular in the 1930s, but are used in a more sophisticated and integrated manner.

Following pages: With the completed Research Tower, the office complex presents a rich and dynamic urban form.

Photographs above and on pages 121–122 are Copyright © 2008 Paul Rocheleau. Photograph opposite is Courtesy The Frank Lloyd Wright Foundation, Taliesin West, Scottsdale, AZ.

Taliesin West

Scottsdale, Arizona, 1937

In the Arizona desert, Wright designed a second architectural community for himself, his family, and his apprentices. Like Taliesin North in Wisconsin, it included offices, drafting rooms, residences, dining and living areas, theaters, service buildings, and gardens. The desert geometries, forms, and materials he used were markedly different from those in green Wisconsin, started two decades before.

Right, top: The form of the drafting room at left contrasts with living areas at right.
Right, bottom: A trellis creates a processional entrance.
Far right: The bell tower links the drafting room with living areas.

Wright's office work area demonstrates Taliesin West's formal motif: strong concrete
walls rising from the desert floor contrast with a light-weight roof of wood and (originally) canvas.
Wright's apprentices collected boulders from the desert to embed in the concrete walls.

Above: Views of the office and drafting room areas. The wide-based concrete walls
were poured on the stable desert sand, with little foundation, but their sloped walls gave them stability.
Opposite: Entrance trellis along drafting room.

Above and opposite: Drafting room. Dramatic diagonals became a unifying element
in both the broad master plan and the forms of individual structures.

Above and right: Terraces, pools, and gardens between the buildings
became a major element of communal life at Taliesin.

Above and left: Dining room and terrace are closely related.

At Taliesin West, Wright invented a new vocabulary of forms for the open desert site.
In many ways their bold geometric shapes derived from the rugged forms of rocks and mountains.
Wood accents provide a contrast.

Mr. and Mrs. Wright's living areas threaded open-air gardens through the enclosed areas. Natural daylight illumined the spaces.

Above, left: The fireplace becomes an integral part of the room space.

Right, top: Indirect lighting provides balanced natural illumination. Right, bottom, and opposite: Wright furniture designs carry out the complex geometries of the architecture and the plan.

Above and opposite: Residential units for Wright's family and apprentices were part of the Taliesin complex.

Above and opposite: Musical performances, dance recitals, lectures, and movies were part of Taliesin life from the beginning.
The Music Pavilion Theater with a luminous ceiling is one of the venues in the complex.

The Cabaret Theater (above) is approached by the long corridor (opposite).

Above: Seating within the theater includes benches and cabaret tables. A triangular motif is repeated in windows and piano alcove.

Opposite: The concrete roof is ornament with lights. Following pages: Bell tower and loggia at residential wing.

NO VISITORS
BEYOND THIS POINT

Florida Southern College

Lakeland, Florida, 1937-54

Wright's largest collection of constructed buildings, planned as a single multi-faceted community, stands at Florida Southern College. Designed as his career revived in the late 1930s, it represents his sprawling, decentralized, yet unified concept of community design. Unlike Mies van der Rohe's contemporaneous Illinois Institute of Technology campus buildings, each of Wright's buildings has a distinct form. Materials, responses to the climate, and the geometry of the entire campus plan bring them together.

Right, top: Science and Cosmography Building, 1953.
Right, bottom: E. T. Roux Library, 1941.
Far right: Roux Library, with semi-circular reading room at left.

Above, left: Lobby of library with skylights, now used for administration.

Above, right, top: The original reading room of the library. Above, right, bottom: Wide-topped concrete columns

form a colonnade. Opposite: Roux Library.

Above, opposite, and following pages: In the hot Florida climate, broad canopies connect each of the Wright buildings. They create
shaded breezeways through the landscaped grounds as Wright's answer to the crowded sidewalks of the traditional city.
The broad marquees are cantilevered from the cast concrete columns. Where the land slopes, the canopies zig-zag up or down as necessary.
Next page: The canopy's Organic geometries and rich ornament unite the campus visually.

Above and opposite: Administration Building, 1945. Opposite: Though altered from Wright's original design, the fountains surrounded by a broad terrace next to the administration buildings create a central focus for community activity.

Industrial Arts Building, 1942. Originally designed as the student center for the 800-student campus, this building's purpose was changed in 1952 when it was built. Above: The relationship of the communal esplanades to the individual buildings shows the organic continuity of the overall design. Opposite: Clerestory windows are framed by cast concrete columns.

Above and opposite: William H. Danforth Chapel, 1954. This second, smaller chapel was built for the church-related college.
Opposite: Leaded glass windows were designed by Wright.

Above and opposite: Ann Merner Pfeiffer Chapel, 1938. The college's main chapel also
served as the college meeting hall. Above: Concrete block inset with colored glass forms a diaphanous wall.
Opposite: A tall, longitudinal bell tower and skylight crowns the building.

Above and opposite: Views of the hexagonal-plan chapel. Second-story balconies
elaborate on the dominant geometry.

Above: Skylight with bell tower above. Opposite: Pfeiffer Chapel's altar, with skylight above.

Above: Skylight with balcony below. Opposite: Organ loft above altar.
Following pages: Stairwell enclosure with embedded colored glass dematerializing the wall.

Kansas City Community Christian Church

Kansas City, Missouri, 1940

Wright's large public buildings designed around 1940 show a wide range of ideas and forms, as here at the Kansas City Community Christian Church.

Right, top: The Kansas City Community Christian Church overlooks the posh Country Club Plaza district, an innovative suburban shopping and residential district begun a decade before. Like the Guggenheim Museum (designed shortly after the church) the building's lines are bold, horizontal, and embrace complex asymmetries.
Right, bottom: The chapel is on the ground floor.
Far right: The main sanctuary has amphitheater seating. Compare the distinctive geometry of the screen and skylights over the altar to those at Florida Southern's Pfeiffer Chapel. The difficult construction of this church, near the beginning of the Second World War, did not achieve the level of quality the design deserved.

Above, left: Stained glass. Above, right: The lobby unites the main sanctuary at right with the spiral stairway at center, which unites each level of the building with the planned roof terrace.
Opposite: A truncated version of the original design's tower can be seen on the roof.

Unitarian Meeting House

Shorewood Hills, Wisconsin, 1947

Right, top, and bottom: The low-slung roof and wide eaves of the entry side blended well with the church's suburban location.

Far right: One of Wright's most widely imitated designs for a public building, the simple, evocative, and modern appearance of the Unitarian Meeting House was echoed by architects across the country.

Clockwise from upper left: As did the designs of Wright's houses of this period, the meeting room space and lobby flowed
easily into each other; corridors and administrative spaces also had a comfortably residential scale; the surprisingly complex spatial
geometry moved from low hearth room space at the rear up to the great window behind the altar. Opposite: Altar.

Above: Main window. Left: Seams of copper-clad roof provide functional ornament that emphasize the structural and symbolic lines of the building. The building repeats the common Wrightian motif of a solid masonry foundation growing out of the ground, with a light, well-engineered roof poised above it. Following pages: Parallelogram chimney (a frequent Wright motif) marks the primary entry into the hearth room/lobby.

V. C. Morris Gift Shop

San Francisco, California, 1948

A rare Wright design for a prototypical urban
site: a downtown San Francisco street.

Right: The brick archway becomes a glass
tunnel introducing the distinctly non-urban
interior space.
Below: Ceramic plaque, colored his favored
Cherokee Red, with Wright's signature.
Far right: Rising directly from the sidewalk, the
V. C. Morris Gift Shop repeats the flat facades
of its neighbors.

Above, right: A spiral ramp defines the interior's curving space. Above, left, top: Side spaces feature low ceilings to contrast with the two-story central space. Above, left, bottom: Soft curves of dropped soffit hide indirect lighting and echo the curvilinear character of the interior. Opposite: Glass entry is seen at right.

Above, left: Built-in cabinetry emphasizes the scale, proportions, and organization Wright intended.
Above, right: Translucent block (with Wright's trademark right-angled spiral) let light in from exterior facade.
Opposite: Side space.

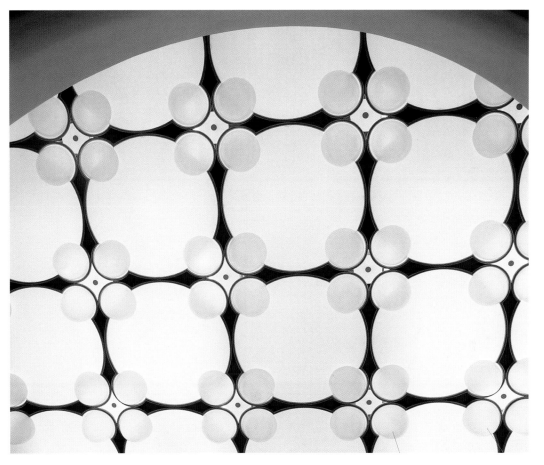

Above, left: Circular niches in ramp wall display shop products.
Above, right: The ceiling adds its own ornamental pattern to the space. Opposite: The luminous ceiling
of translucent circles and hemispheres helps to extend the space vertically.

Price Tower

Bartlesville, Oklahoma, 1952

In Wright's prototypical city, Broadacres, skyscrapers would stand free from other tall buildings, as does the Price Tower.

Far right: Lobby of Price Tower penthouse office.

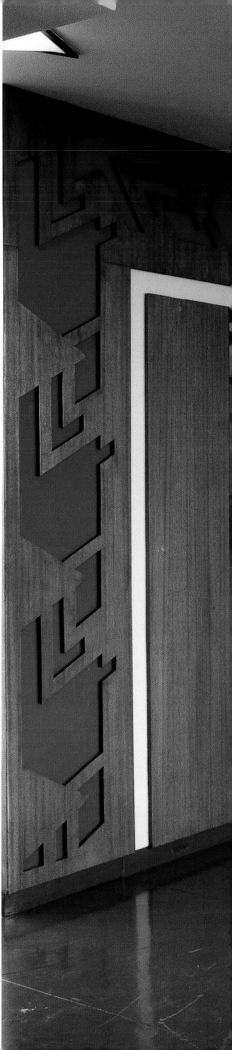

Above: Views of the penthouse office of Harold Price, Sr., showing built-in furniture, fireplace, balcony, and ornamental mural. Opposite: Reception and secretary's area.

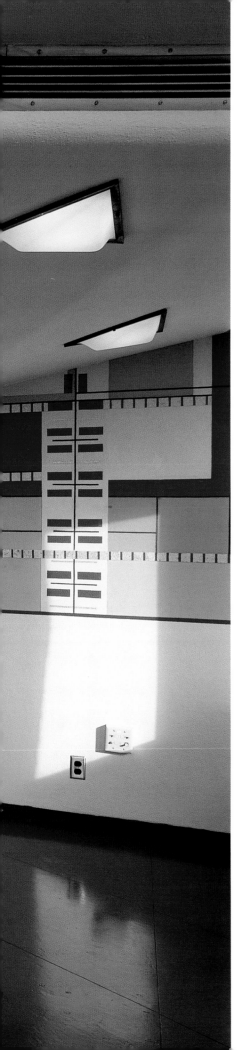

Left: A typical living room of two-story apartments in tower, including fireplace.
Above, top: View from living room. Above, bottom: Detail of ornamental mural, inscribed by Wright.

Each apartment has a mezzanine. Top: Copper trim on balcony edge, echoing exterior copper cladding.
Above, left: Bathroom. Above, right: Kitchen. Opposite: Living room. From left, dining table, door to kitchen,
door to powder room, stairs to two bedrooms upstairs, and front door beyond couch.

Above, left: Exterior facade, showing horizontal copper louvered sunshades.

Above, right: Penthouse with office of Harold Price, Sr. Opposite: View from bedroom balcony.

Vertical copper sunscreens line exterior of apartments.

Anderton Court

Beverly Hills, California, 1952

In contrast to the V. C. Morris Gift Shop, Anderton Court shops are closer to Wright's progressive vision of a new kind of city.

Right: Most of the facade is expressed in glass; the spiral circulation ramp is the main feature of the architecture.
Far right: The open-air ramp brings light and air into the center of the building.

Above: Columns, doors, and slanting glass walls all express the design's unifying, angular aesthetic.

Opposite: An ultramodern spire becomes a sign for the shops. Individual stores are set off the ramp.

Beth Sholom Synagogue

Elkins Park, Pennsylvania, 1954

In Broadacre City, the adventurous silhouettes of major public buildings like Beth Sholom Synagogue would become the city's landmarks. Wright intended them to be as memorable as, though radically different from, the spires and domes of traditional cities.

Right: Aluminum and glass clad the exterior. Far right: Derived from a tripod steel structural concept, the mountain-like form also expressed religious symbolism.

Above: The aluminum roof sits on a bowl-like concrete structure.

Left: The translucent roof is radiant by day and glowing by night.

Above, left: Entry. Above, right: Detail of foundation. Opposite: Altar, main sanctuary.

Above: Sisterhood Sanctuary on ground floor. Right: The floor, like the roof, is angled in planes.
The double-paned roof is glass on the exterior, fiberglass on the interior.

Kalita Humphreys Theater

Dallas, Texas, 1955

The Kalita Humphreys Theater represents a
clean yet rich urban architecture. The emphasis
is horizontal, in keeping with the lines of
Wright's ideal, Broadacre City. The cylindrical fly
tower stands over the circular revolving stage.

Right, top: The building responds to the
topography of the site.
Right, bottom: Clerestory windows allow
continuous light.
Far right: Main entry.

Above, top: Inverted forms rise from a narrow base to wider upper floors in the cantilevered concrete structure.
Above, bottom: Functional light fixtures also act as ornament. Left: The ornamentation and shape of tapering columns define their distinct function in the structure, while the ceiling plane helps to blend the interior and exterior into one space.

Above and right: Irregular terraced seating wraps around the circular stage.
The stage revolved so that one scene could be assembled while another was in use.

Karl Kundert Medical Clinic

San Luis Obispo, California, 1955

A series of medical clinics built across the
United States allowed Wright to show how
smaller public buildings would fit into the
suburban landscape he advocated. Most were
based on the scale, forms, and plans of his
Usonian houses, adapted to medical office
needs.

Right: Clerestory windows are screened with
ornamental cut-outs based on Organic motifs.
Far right: Horizontal Usonian form is accented
by a raised space over the waiting room.

Above: The public side of the building turns a mostly blank brick wall to the street. Opposite: Like many
Wright houses, the clinic is set on a dramatic natural site overlooking a stream, allowing terraces and plantings to be incorporated.
Following pages: The stream side of the building brings light and views into the building.

Kenneth L. Meyers Medical Clinic

Dayton, Ohio, 1956

Right, top: Entry shows how this building blends with its suburban environment.
Right, bottom: Waiting room (also shown at far right) is at left in this photograph.
Far right: Waiting room takes the place of the living room in a Usonian house, but otherwise uses balanced lighting and a contrast of natural materials to create the space.

Following pages: Glass doors and walls open the garden side to light and views, just like a Usonian house.

Solomon R. Guggenheim Museum

New York, New York, 1956

The Guggenheim may be Wright's ultimate statement of urbanism. While its Organic forms repudiate the conventional urban forms of twentieth century America, they also confidently proclaim the free forms, open spaces, and horizontal expanse of his ideal, Broadacre City.

Right: Wright designed the Guggenheim to stand in extreme contrast to the crowded, vertical skyscrapers and rectilinear street grids of Manhattan. The Guggenheim's broad horizontal lines echo the Kansas City Community Church, also designed in the early 1940s. Smaller galleries are in lower wing at left, entry is at center, and the main gallery is within the spiral at right.

Drawing of Frank Lloyd Wright is Copyright © 2008 The Frank Lloyd Wright Foundation, Taliesin West, Scottsdale, AZ.

Opposite: Responding to Wright's acceptance of the auto, the entry was originally a drive-through porte-cochere. Slits dividing bands in the main gallery hold windows for natural lighting.

Credit: The Solomon R. Guggenheim Museum, New York.

Photography by William H. Short © Solomon R. Guggenheim Foundation, New York.

THE MODERN GALLERY
MUSEUM FOR THE SOLOMON R GUGGENHEIM FOUNDATION
FRANK LLOYD WRIGHT ARCHITECT
HOLDEN AND McLAUGHLIN ASSOCIATES

Above: The spirals allow visitors to view art featured in the museum from many angles and distances.
Right: Entry.
Left: Spiral ramps circle the drum of the main gallery. The exhibit shown is a 2008 installation by Cai Guo-Qiang.

Above and right: Smaller galleries are contained in the lower wing.
Opposite: A triangular stairway links the museum floors.

Above and left: Auditorium on lower level, beneath the main gallery.

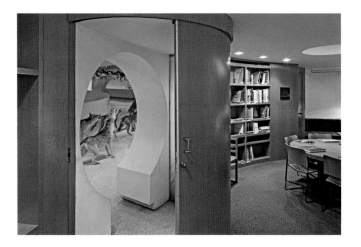

Above: Gallery off main ramp.

Right: Wright intended for visitors to take elevators to the top floor, and then walk at a comfortable downhill pace to observe the art mounted on the perimeter walls.

Credit: Installation view of the exhibition *David Smith: A Centennial* at the Solomon R. Guggenheim Museum, New York, 2006. Photograph by David Heald © The Solomon R. Guggenheim Foundation.

Above: Wide ramps accommodate both circulation and room to observe the art. The building shows Wright's desire to re-invent conventional architectural solutions.

Left: View of main gallery from above. Credit: Installation view of the exhibition *David Smith: A Centennial* at the Solomon R. Guggenheim Museum, New York, 2006. Photograph by David Heald © The Solomon R. Guggenheim Foundation.

Above: Vertical fin walls divide the perimeter wall space into discrete areas for viewing art.

Above: Service core at right holds stairs and elevators.

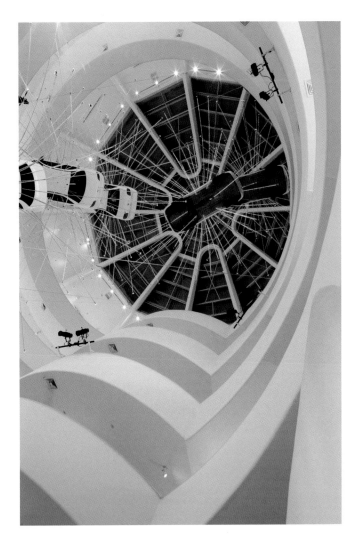

Above and right: As in the Marin County Civic Center and the Kansas City Community Christian Church, Wright opens the center of the building to sunlight. The large skylight (seen here at night) that tops the main space has its own bold ornamental form to complement the simple lines of the curving balconies.

Top: View from ground floor up to skylight. Above: View from upper
balcony down to ground floor, including the small pool and fountain at lower right.

Left: View of skylight and upper ramps. Credit: Interior of the Solomon R. Guggenheim Museum, New York.
Photograph by David Heald © The Solomon R. Guggenheim Foundation.

R.W. Lindholm Service Station

Cloquet, Minnesota, 1956

Wright embraced the automobile and its architecture with more enthusiasm and understanding than most Modern architects of his era. This gas station (the only one of Wright's design that was built) demonstrates how he interpreted a roadside building's need for prominent signage and practical service into a logical and aesthetic form.

Right: Rather than having pumps sitting on the ground, Wright expected to have gas hoses suspended from the cantilevered canopy. Building codes did not allow this idea to be put into use.

Far right: The shield-shaped Phillips 66 sign is not by Wright; the tall spire-sign with original lettering was his design.

Wright saw service stations as natural rest stops in the bustling city. Above: Service bays for cars extend at left. An office is on the ground floor. Left: The second-story lounge is elevated to permit easy observation of the entire station.

Marin County Civic Center

San Rafael, California, 1957

The largest public building Wright built (completed after his death in 1959) serves as the virtual Capitol of Broadacre City. It summarizes his fundamental urban ideas: mated to nature, shaped logically by the automobile, symbolizing a decentralized democracy, and using an original Organic vocabulary of forms and decoration.

Right: The thrusting prow of the administration wing (left) features a hanging garden and a gold anodized aluminum broadcast tower and chimney.

Following pages: The long structure spans three small hills, with the courthouse wing at left, the library in the central dome, and the administrative wing at right.

Above and right: Two views of the central dome. Roof is cast concrete. The original color was to be gold, but a paint that would hold the color without fading could not be found. The Board of Supervisors chambers are at the base of the dome, with doors letting out onto terraces and views.

Far right: Screen walls and wide eaves shade the glass walls of the offices.

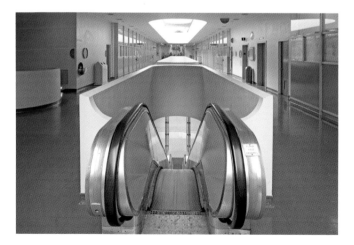

Above, top: Bridge and lobby entry to courthouse wing. Globe lights echo the gold anodized globes lining the eaves. Above, middle and bottom: Escalators lead up from the ground floor through the central light atrium to the upper levels. These open-air corridors connect the building's offices and courts. Left: The building's two wings create bridges, allowing cars to drive through the building for easy access throughout the site.

LIBRAR

Above: A modular system of glass and steel walls, doors, and windows allows light from the central light well into all offices.
Right: A shallow dome tops the library, with book stacks ranging radially around the edge.
Left: Skylight over open-air balconies; the library is at top, at the center of the building, symbolizing democracy's reliance on knowledge.

Above: Wright designed the interior corridor to have the same openness and architectural details as the exterior of the building, blurring the distinction between indoors and out. The skylights are not part of Wright's original design.
Right: Interior planting further creates the sense of being in the middle of nature. The far end of the corridor leads directly out onto the hillside.
Far right: The light well looks down to car drive through the ground floor of the building.

Above: Public cafeteria.
Left: Corridor outside public cafeteria.
Opposite, top: Hanging gardens off cafeteria on terraced prow.
Opposite, left: Hanging gardens. Pool cascades through wall, leading symbolically to the bay in distance.
Opposite, right: Prow with water pouring through scupper.

Wright planned theaters, exhibition halls, and other public facilities at the civic center
so that it would become a true suburban center. Left: Exhibit hall, designed by
Taliesin Associated Architects, 1975. Wright colleague Aaron Green supervised the development
of the Marin County Civic Center after Wright's death. Above: Circular forms and globe
ornamental fixtures carry on the civic center's design themes.

Veterans' Auditorium, designed by Taliesin Associated Architects, 1972.
Above: Entry. Bottom: Fly loft of auditorium. Right: Sculptured, blue-painted concrete
roof carries on the scale and look of the civic center.

Left: Wright designed this United States Post Office for the civic center.
It is the only building for the federal government that he ever built.
The structure is concrete block. Above: Service buildings for civic center.
Following pages: The artificial lake was intended by Wright to mirror
the building's response to the natural setting.

Juvenile Cultural Study Center

Wichita State University, Wichita, Kansas, 1957

The Juvenile Cultural Study Center is a complex of classrooms and offices for Wichita State University's education department.

Right, above: Roof terrace.
Right, bottom: Pools and fountains are a frequent Wright motif that introduce nature into a building.
Far right: Two wings flank a central court with a fountain. Classrooms are at left, offices at right.

Above: Light, decorative spires, and circles contrast with the rectilinear lines of the structure. Opposite: One of two symmetrical outdoor courts is sheltered by tall monitors. Following pages: Indoor and outdoor spaces, ground-floor courtyards, and roof terraces create a complex interplay of spaces and structure in this design.

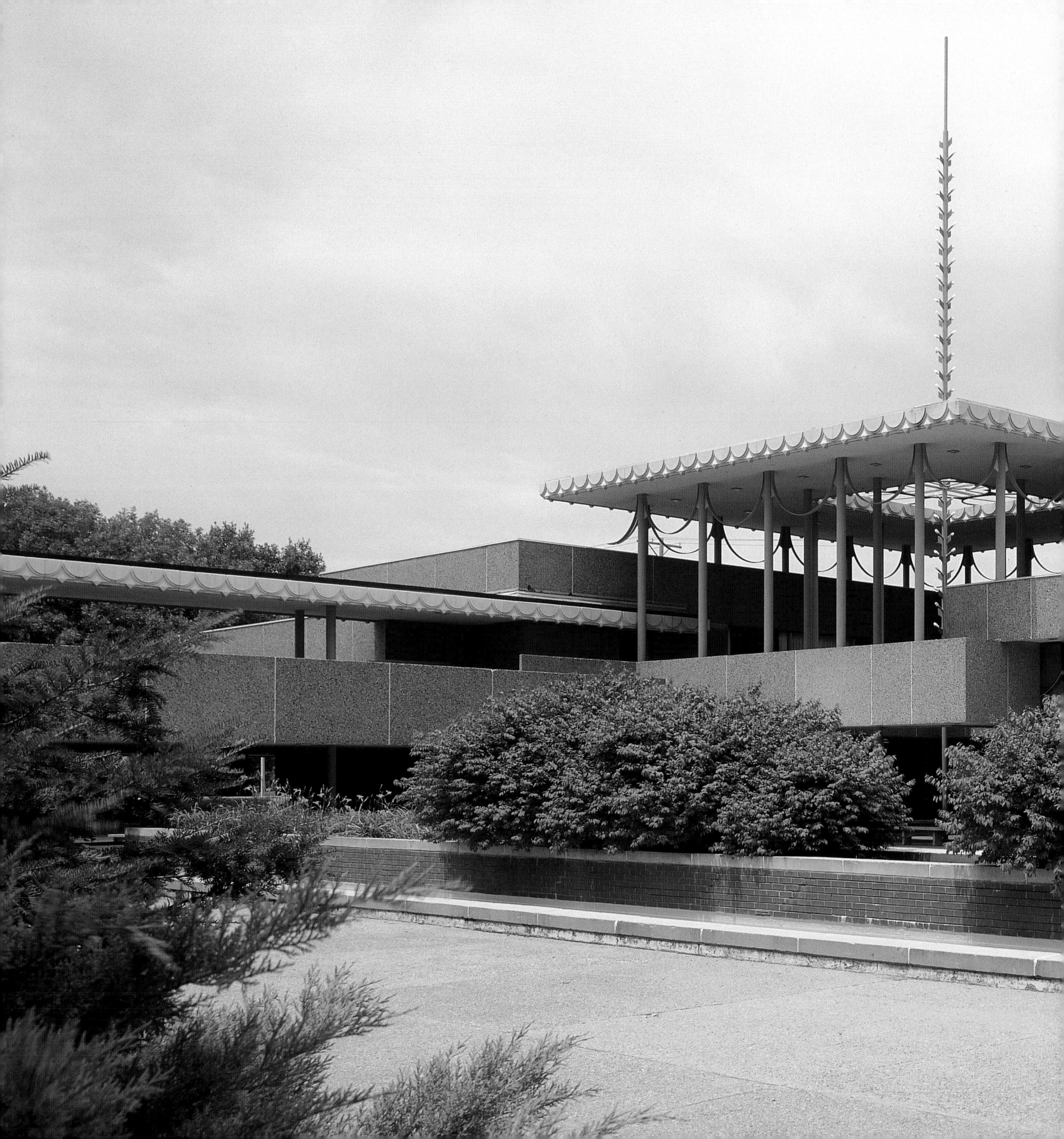

Pilgrim Congregational Church

Redding, California, 1958

Right, top: The church's blue-roofed
fellowship hall and sanctuary is seen beyond
the low classroom wing with play yard.
Right, bottom: entry. The roof is suspended
from concrete beams.
Far right: The sanctuary wing has a porch.
A basement level is below.

Above: The exposed structure creates the rhythmic and formal aesthetic of the design.
Left: The main sanctuary and a chapel, never built, were to stand to the right of the fellowship hall
and its blue roof.

The fellowship hall has become the main sanctuary for the church.

Above, left: A fireplace stands next to the altar. Above, right: Desert stone walls focus on natural materials.

Opposite: The Douglas fir ceiling was originally intended to be of redwood poles.

Grady Gammage Memorial Auditorium

Arizona State University,
Tempe, Arizona, 1959

Like Marin County Civic Center, Gammage
Auditorium reflects Wright's concept for large civic
monuments, which were to give focus and
identity to Broadacre City. The ground-floor lobby
behind glass windows sits below the open-air
terrace on the second floor. Ramps extending out
to the parking lot can be seen at right and left.

Above: Brick wings enclose circulation ramps and backstage areas, carrying on the circular geometry of the building.
Right: Ramps.
Left: Ramps leading down from upper level are ornamented with arches and lights.

Above, top: Entry plaza. Above, middle: Main foyer.
Above, bottom: Ticket booth. The circular motif of the building's plan is echoed
in the shape of each element. Left: Lobby and ticket booth.

Above: Interior ramp.
Right: Ramps to upper level.
Far right: An open-air terrace at second level.

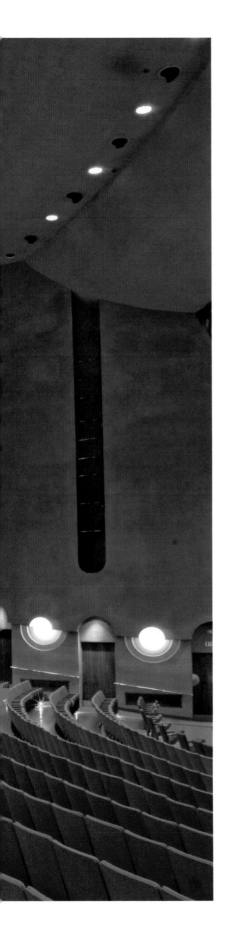

Above: Side aisle.
Right: Entry to auditorium.
Left: Auditorium. Instead of radial aisles, Wright used continental seating, leaving space between each row for others to pass seated patrons comfortably.

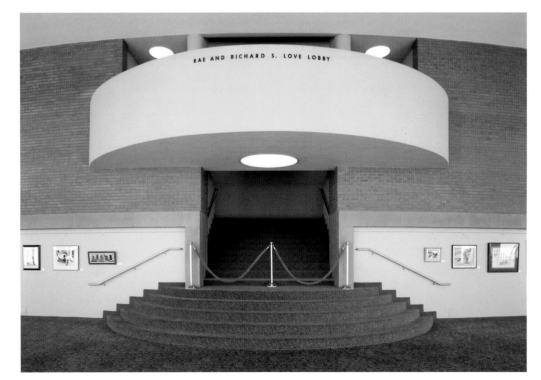

Above, right, far right:
Views of auditorium interior
and its two balconies. The
auditorium holds 3,000
people. The first balcony (at
far right), or grand tier, is
suspended apart from the
rear wall, creating a fuller
acoustic space.
Following pages: The stage.

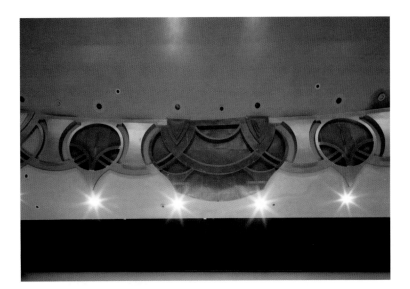

Above, top: Decoration. Above, bottom: View from balcony to stage.
Left: Upper balcony. Following pages: View of suspended grand tier balcony.
The broad shapes and small details of the building fit into a common
geometrical aesthetic, a hallmark of Wright's Organic architecture.

BUILDINGS LIST

Constructed public buildings
by Frank Lloyd Wright

1886

Unity Chapel
Spring Green, Wisconsin

1887

Hillside Home School
Spring Green, Wisconsin

1893

Municipal Boathouse,
Lake Mendota
Madison, Wisconsin

1896

Romeo and Juliet Windmill
Spring Green, Wisconsin

1897

Frank Lloyd Wright Studio
Oak Park, Illinois

1898

River Forest Golf Club
River Forest, Illinois

1901

Buffalo Exposition Pavilion,
Universal Portland Cement Co.
Buffalo, New York

1902

Hillside Home School II
Spring Green, Wisconsin

Lake Delavan Yacht Club
Delavan, Wisconsin

1903

Larkin Company Administration
Building
Buffalo, New York

Abraham Lincoln Center
Chicago, Illinois

Scoville Park Fountain
Oak Park, Illinois

1904

Unity Temple
Oak Park, Illinois

1905

E. W. Cummings Real Estate Office
River Forest, Illinois

E-Z Polish Factory
Chicago, Illinois

Lawrence Memorial Library
Springfield, Illinois

Rookery Building Lobby
Chicago, Illinois

Frank L. Smith Bank
Dwight, Illinois

1906

William H. Pettit Memorial Chapel
Belvidere, Illinois

River Forest Tennis Club
River Forest, Illinois

1907

Fox River Country Club Addition
Geneva, Illinois

Jamestown Exhibition Pavilion,
Larkin Company
Norfolk, Virginia

Pebbles & Balch Shop
Oak Park, Illinois

1908

Bitter Root Inn
Bitter Root, Montana

Browne's Bookstore
Chicago, Illinois

1909

City National Bank Building
and Park Inn Hotel
Mason City, Iowa

Como Orchard Summer Colony
Darby, Montana

W. Scott Thurber Art Gallery
Chicago, Illinois

Peter C. Stohr Arcade Building
Chicago, Illinois

1910

New York Exhibition Building,
Universal Portland Cement Co.
New York, New York

1911

Banff National Park Pavilion
Alberta, Canada

Lake Geneva Hotel
Lake Geneva, Wisconsin

Taliesin North
Spring Green, Wisconsin

1912

**Observation Platform,
Island Woolen Mills**
Baraboo, Wisconsin

Park Ridge Country Club
Park Ridge, Illinois

1913

Midway Gardens
Chicago, Illinois

1914

Mori Oriental Art Studio
Chicago, Illinois

**Women's Building,
Inter-County Fair Grounds**
Spring Green, Wisconsin

1915

A. D. German Warehouse
Richland Center, Wisconsin

Imperial Hotel
Tokyo, Japan

1921

Jiyu Gakuen Girls' School
Tokyo, Japan

1927
Arizona Biltmore Hotel
Phoenix, Arizona
(consultant to Albert McArthur,
architect)

1928

Ocatillo Desert Camp
Chandler, Arizona

1932

**Taliesin Fellowship Complex
additions**
Spring Green, Wisconsin

1936

**S. C. Johnson & Son
Administration Building**
Racine, Wisconsin

1937

Edgar J. Kaufmann, Sr., Office
Pittsburgh, Pennsylvania

Taliesin West
Scottsdale, Arizona

1938

Florida Southern College
Lakeland, Florida

Midway Barns
Spring Green, Wisconsin

1940

Community Christian Church
Kansas City, Missouri

1944

**S. C. Johnson & Son
Research Tower**
Racine, Wisconsin

1947

Unitarian Meeting House
Shorewood Hills, Wisconsin

1948

V. C. Morris Gift Shop
San Francisco, California

1951

**Aaron Green-Frank Lloyd Wright
Field Office**
San Francisco, California

1952

Anderton Court Shops
Beverly Hills, California

Price Company Tower
Bartlesville, Oklahoma

1953

Riverview Terrace Restaurant
Spring Green, Wisconsin

1954

Beth Sholom Synagogue
Elkins Park, Pennsylvania

Hoffman Auto Showroom
New York, New York

Municipal Art Gallery
Los Angeles, California

1955

Kalita Humphreys Theater
Dallas, Texas

Karl Kundert Medical Clinic
San Luis Obispo, California

1956

**Annunciation Greek Orthodox
Church**
Wauwatosa, Wisconsin

Solomon R. Guggenheim Museum
New York, New York

R. W. Lindholm Service Station
Cloquet, Minnesota

Kenneth L. Meyers Medical Clinic
Dayton, Ohio

Wyoming Valley Grammar School
Wyoming Valley, Wisconsin

1957

Herman T. Fasbender Medical Clinic
Hastings, Minnesota

Juvenile Cultural Study Center
Wichita State University,
Wichita, Kansas

Lockridge Medical Clinic
Whitefish, Montana

Marin County Civic Center
San Rafael, California

1958

Pilgrim Congregational Church
Redding, California

1959

**Grady Gammage Memorial
Auditorium**
Arizona State University,
Tempe, Arizona

ENDNOTES

Frank Lloyd Wright: Buildings for the City
By Alan Hess

1 Frank Lloyd Wright. *The Living City* (New York: Horizon Press, Inc., 1958), pp. 59–60.

2 Ibid., p. 97.

3 Neil Levine. *The Architecture of Frank Lloyd Wright* (Princeton, NJ: Princeton University Press, 1996), pp. xiv, 422–423.

4 Wright, p. 115.

5 Ibid., p. 233.

6 Ibid., p. 98.

7 Wright dated the St. Mark's Apartment designs variously as 1921, 1922, and 1925.

8 Wright, p. 27.

9 Ibid., p. 83.

10 Ibid., p. 39.

11 Ibid., p. 228.

12 Ibid., pp. 19–20.

13 Ibid., p. 85.

14 Ibid., p. 22.

15 Ibid., p. 24.

16 Ibid., p. 26.

17 Ibid., p. 86.

18 Ibid., p. 203.

19 Ibid., p. 22.

20 Ibid., p. 187.

21 It is interesting that Wright's progressive suggestion was the same that General Motors implemented in practice as they replaced aging streetcar systems with internal combustion buses—thereby launching the urban legend that they destroyed efficient mass rail transit solely for their own profit.

22 Wright., p. 125.

23 Ibid., p. 185.

24 Ibid., p. 186.

25 Ibid., p. 110. Ironically Wright applied this metaphor of disease to the existing city circa 1950; the same metaphor has since been appropriated by critics of suburban decentralization and "sprawl."

26 Ibid., p. 53.

Reshaping Urban Landscapes
By David G. De Long

1 The project is described in Bruce Brooks Pfeiffer, *Treasures of Taliesin* (San Francisco: Pomegranate Press, 1999), p. 12.

2 The project is described in Frank Lloyd Wright, *Frank Lloyd Wright*, edited and photographed by Yukio Futagawa, text by Bruce Brooks Pfeiffer, 12 volumes (title varies; Tokyo: A.D.A. Edita, 1984–88), vol. 1, pp. 122–123.

3 These designs should not be confused with his less structured proposals for community layouts, in which he worked variations on orthogonal grids, beginning with an 1896 proposal (unbuilt) for Charles Roberts in what would become Oak Park, Illinois, as discussed by Neil Levine, "The Quadruple Block Plan and Frank Lloyd Wright's Obsession with the Grid," *eaV* (Versailles Architecture Journal No. 11, 2005/2006), pp. 62–84. These led to designs for Broadacre City, designed for a hypothetical site, in which Wright related his design to the grid of the nation's platted section lines, as discussed in David G. De Long, "Frank Lloyd Wright and the Evolution of the Living City," in *Frank Lloyd Wright and the Living City*, edited by David G. De Long (Weil am Rhein, Germany, and Milan: Vitra Design Museum in association with Skira editore, 1998), pp. 15–69.

4 Among the first to note this was Henry-Russell Hitchcock, "Frank Lloyd Wright and the 'Academic Tradition' of the Early Eighteen-Nineties," *Journal of the Warburg and Courtauld Institutes* 8 (January – June, 1944), pp. 46–63.

5 Frank Lloyd Wright, "In the Cause of Architecture" (1908), reprinted in Wright, *Collected Writings*, vol. 1, p. 94.

6 As discussed, in David G. De Long, "Frank Lloyd Wright: Designs for an American Landscape, 1922–1932," in *Frank Lloyd Wright: Designs for an American Landscape, 1922–1932* (Harry N. Abrams in association with the Canadian Centre for Architecture, the Library of Congress, and the Frank Lloyd Wright Foundation, 1996), pp. 16–47. Also, Robert L. Sweeney, *Wright in Hollywood: Visions of a New Architecture* (New York, Cambridge, Mass., and London: the Architectural History Foundation in association with the MIT Press, 1994), pp. 10–19.

7 Frank Lloyd Wright, *The Living City* (New York: Horizon Press, 1958), p. 144.

8 Frank Lloyd Wright, *The Natural House* (1954), reprinted in Wright, *Collected Writings*, vol. 5, p. 112.

9 As discussed in De Long, *Designs for an American Landscape*, pp. 100–114. Also, Sweeney, *Wright in Hollywood*, pp. 140–165.

10 Frank Lloyd Wright on the Hanna House in *The Architectural Forum* (1938), reprinted in Wright, *Collected Writings*, vol. 3, p. 283.

11 Pfeiffer, *Treasures of Taliesin*, pp. 50–51. The colleagues cited are P.G. Grove, a contractor, and Franz Aust, a landscape architect affiliated with the University of Wisconsin in Madison.

12 Bruce Brooks Pfeiffer, editorial text in Wright, *Frank Lloyd Wright*, vol. 6, pp. 100–103.

13 As described in De Long, *Designs for an American Landscape*, pp. 80–100.

14 The project is described in Pfeiffer, *Treasures of Taliesin*, pp. 54–66.

15 The commission is described in Pfeiffer, *Treasures of Taliesin*, pp. 91–97.

16 Interest in Wright's Baghdad project has revived, as reported by Adam Cohen, "Building for Democracy," *The Wall Street Journal* (August 20, 2003), editorial page; and Sam Lubell, "Frank Lloyd Wright's 1957 Plans for Baghdad Back in the Limelight," *Architectural Record* 191 (September 2003), p. 46. Mina Marefat, while a Rockefeller Scholar at the John W. Kluge Center at the Library of Congress in 2003, was pursuing studies of the project.

17 The design in question was Goff's first proposal for the Joe Price studio (Bartlesville, Oklahoma, 1953; unbuilt), as discussed, together with the text of Wright's criticism, in David G. De Long, *Bruce Goff: Toward Absolute Architecture* (New York, Cambridge, Mass., and London: The Architectural History Foundation in association with the MIT Press, 1988), pp. 122–131.

BIBLIOGRAPHY

Friedland, Roger and Harold Zellman. *The Fellowship: The Untold Story of Frank Lloyd Wright & The Taliesin Fellowship*. New York: HarperCollins Publishers, 2006.

Gill, Brendan. *Many Masks: A Life of Frank Lloyd Wright*. New York: Ballantine Books, 1987.

Green, Aaron and Donald P. De Nevi. *An Architecture for Democracy: The Marin County Civic Center*. San Francisco: Grendon Publishing, 1990.

Hitchcock, Henry-Russell. *In the Nature of Materials*. New York: Hawthorn Books, 1942.

Izzo, Alberto and Camillo Gubitosi. *Frank Lloyd Wright: Drawings 1887–1959*. London: Academy Editions, 1977.

Levine, Neil. *The Architecture of Frank Lloyd Wright*. Princeton, N. J. : Princeton University Press, 1996.

Manson, Grant. *Frank Lloyd Wright to 1910: The First Golden Age*. New York: Reinhold, 1958.

Pfeiffer, Bruce Brooks and Gerald Nordland, eds. *Frank Lloyd Wright: In the Realm of Ideas*. Carbondale, IL: Southern Illinois University Press, 1988.

Pfeiffer, Bruce Brooks, ed. *Frank Lloyd Wright: Collected Writings*. New York: Rizzoli International Publications, 1995.

Scully, Vincent. *Frank Lloyd Wright*. New York: George Braziller, 1960.

Secrest, Meryle. *Frank Lloyd Wright: A Biography*. New York: Alfred A. Knopf, 1992.

Smith, Kathryn. *Frank Lloyd Wright: Hollyhock House and Olive Hill*. New York: Rizzoli International Publications, 1992.

Smith, Kathryn, and Peter Reed and William Kazain, eds. *The Show to End All Shows: Frank Lloyd Wright and the Museum of Modern Art, 1940*. New York: Museum of Modern Art, 2005.

Storrer, William Allin. *The Architecture of Frank Lloyd Wright: A Complete Catalog*. Chicago: University of Chicago Press, 2002.

Storrer, William Allin. *The Frank Lloyd Wright Companion*. Chicago: The University of Chicago Press.

Sweeney, Robert L. *Wright in Hollywood: Visions of a New Architecture*. New York: Architectural History Foundation, 1994.

Tafel, Edgar. *Apprentice to Genius: Years with Frank Lloyd Wright*. New York: McGraw-Hill Book Co.,1979.

Tafel, Edgar. *About Wright: An Album of Recollections by those who knew Frank Lloyd Wright*. New York: John Wiley and Sons, Inc., 1993.

Twombley, Robert C. *Frank Lloyd Wright: His Life and His Architecture*. New York: John Wiley and Sons, Inc., 1979.

Wright, Frank Lloyd. *An Autobiography*. New York: Horizon Press, 1977.

Wright, Frank Lloyd, and Edgar Kaufmann (ed.) *An American Architecture*. New York: Barnes & Noble, 1998.

Wright, Frank Lloyd. *The Living City*. New York: Horizon Press, Inc., 1958.

INDEX

Note: Numbers in italics refer
to illustrations or photographs.